Don't Talk Frustrated at Me, I'm Beautiful

By Nikki Hughes

♡ Nikki Hughes

For Emma, Ben and Katie

Table of Contents

Preface

My life was forever changed on March 23rd, 2004. At exactly 11:26pm and after thirty hours of labor, my daughter Emma made her grand entrance into the world. When they placed her on my chest the world stood perfectly still. The sounds of the hospital monitors quieted, the bustling of doctors and nurses faded into the woodwork, and the extreme pain I felt was dulled for those few precious moments. She was absolutely beautiful. The tears silently flowed down my cheeks as I felt her little fingers curl around mine. She grabbed my heart with a love so fierce that it almost hurt.

This euphoric feeling was quickly followed by sudden panic. The thoughts came rushing into my head like a freight train: "Am I really responsible for another human being now? I have absolutely no idea how to take care of a baby! Are they going to tell me what to do? What if she cries and I can't help her? How do I feed her? What if I never get to sleep again? *What if I'm not a good mom?*"

I was scared. But the love I felt for Emma quickly overshadowed the doubts creeping into my mind. I remember whispering these words to her that night- "We're in this together for the long haul baby girl. You're stuck with me. I may not know what I'm doing, but I sure love you a lot."

Your journey into motherhood is your own unique story. You may have labored hard at the hospital or at home, cherishing those first cries as you cradled him in your arms. Maybe you flew halfway across the world to hold your daughter for the first time. Maybe you're a mother to a foster child, who desperately needed some loving arms. You may have been handed a precious baby by a social worker, and felt a love so deep you couldn't breathe. You might have married someone with wonderful kids, and are embracing them as your own. Maybe you are a mother to your grandbabies and are praying for the strength to do it all over again.

You may be an auntie, cousin or sister that has humbly stepped forward to fill a void in the life of a child. You might be a momma to babies that are already in the arms of Jesus, and you can't wait for the day you get to hold them again. You might be a single mom working two jobs and doing the very best you can. Maybe you're a teacher who pours her heart and soul into her students every single day- hoping and praying that you are making a difference in their life. Or just maybe you are longing to be a mother and are trying desperately to be patient for God's perfect timing.

We have arrived at motherhood in many different ways. But one thing remains the same: we love our children with every fiber of our being. Whether you are a mom living in the heart of New York City or a mom living in a small village in Uganda, deep down we understand the hearts of each other. You may be waking your kids up at 5:00am to milk the cows on the family farm, or you might be riding the subway with them to school. One mom is kissing her kid's goodnight in Japan while another is waking hers up in Argentina. No matter where we live or what our circumstances are, we are all doing our very best to raise amazing men and women.

But raising kids is not an easy gig. Wonderful? Yes. Fulfilling? Yes. Completely awesome? Yes. But easy? *Absolutely not.* I realized this that very first night in the hospital. And ever since then, it's been a roller coaster ride I wouldn't trade for anything in the world. Full of highs, full of lows, and full of twists and turns that I never even saw coming.

The day I walked into the kitchen and saw my two-year old son flinging our fine china across the room, I knew I needed some mommy back up. When I was up to my ears in diapers and hadn't slept in three days, I needed to hear that this wouldn't last forever. In an attempt to regain some of my sanity back, I began to share my stories. And that's when something very amazing happened- I found out I wasn't alone. People began sharing their stories with me, too. We could laugh together at how *not perfect* we were. And in the still quiet of the night, as I rocked a crying baby back to sleep, I knew there was another mommy out there somewhere doing the exact same thing.

When you're a mom deep in the trenches of potty training and you haven't left the house in days, it's good to know you're not alone. When you have a fight with your daughter and she slams the door in your face, it's good to know you're not alone. When you stand in the kitchen and can't believe you have to make dinner *again*, it's good to know you're not alone. And when you feel like you're failing as a mom, it's good to know you're not alone.

Right now there are mothers all around the world experiencing moments with their kids. Some of these moments will be magical. Some will be so maddening they can't even think straight. Some moments will be hilarious. Some humiliating. Many will be frustrating. Some will be filled with sorrow. And then there will be those moments that take their breath away.

I want to share some of my moments as a mom with you- the good, the bad, and yes, the ugly. We have to be real with each other. We're not perfect and we're never going to be. I thank God every day that kids are so forgiving. They love us even though we make mistakes. I hope that my crazy life strikes a chord with you. Don't be afraid to share your stories- we need each other.

Don't Talk Frustrated at Me, I'm Beautiful

It was a busy afternoon, and I was trying to get the house clean before my older kids got home from school. Meanwhile, my precious three-year old daughter was doing *her* best to *mess up* the whole house. My patience was getting very thin. I would clean a room- she would mess it up. I would put the puzzles away- she would dump them out. I would make the bed- she would pull the covers off to build a fort. She had pushed me to the edge of my sanity.

I walked into her room and found her waist-deep in stuffed animals. "Katie, you need to put all of these toys away right now! I can't even walk in here," I said.

"Okay, mommy," she replied, without taking her eyes off of the Barbie doll in her hand.

"I mean it," I said seriously, "I'm coming back in five minutes and these stuffed animals better be picked up."

"Ok," she said. A few minutes later I went to check on her. There she sat, still playing with her dolls and still oblivious to the mess surrounding her. "Katherine Elizabeth," I said, " you are not obeying me. You need to pick up these toys right now!"

"No tanks, mommy," she said with the hint of a smile, "I'm still playing with them."

I took a deep breath and said sternly, "If you don't obey me right now, you're going to go on time-out!"

She looked up at me with tears in her eyes and said, "Don't talk frustrated at me, I'm beautiful!"

You know you need that Money

When Ben was four years old, he went through a phase where he would not wipe himself. You all know what I'm talking about. He could do it, but it TOTALLY grossed him out. In fact, the whole idea of pooping grossed him out. He would sit there on the toilet with his eyes closed and nose plugged, only coming up for air long enough to yell, "Can somebody come wipe me? And bring the spray!"

This all seemed very bizarre to me. I mean, really? Did he not get that it totally grossed *me* out too? I tried to explain to him that it's *way* grosser to deal with someone else's poop rather than your own. But he wasn't buying it.

So, in an effort to ease him into this harsh reality, we decided that we would help him in the morning (when he apparently couldn't do it without gagging), but he would have to wipe himself in the afternoon.

It was put to the test the very next day. He came running in from outside and yelled, "Mom, I gotta go poop so bad!" So I told him to go- himself. *Alone.*

He pleaded with me, "Mom, I'll give you a quarter if you come help me. I have the money in my piggy bank."

I shook my head and said, "You know the rule. Now go for crying out loud!"

A few minutes later I heard him yelling from the bathroom, "I'm done, Mom. Come help me!"

"You need to do it yourself!" I yelled back.

"Come on, mom, you know you need that money!" He replied.

When your kid tries to negotiate a poop wipe, that's a pretty good sign that he should be doing it himself.

Just Ask Santa

We were driving in the car and I asked the kids what they wanted for Christmas. Emma quickly said, "I really, *really* want the Barbie dreamboat so bad!"

"But Emma," Ben replied, "isn't that like $100 or something?"

"I know, that's why I'm asking Santa for that one," she continued, "it's free then, remember?"

Ben's face lit up with excitement. "That's a great idea! I never thought of that! Mom, we'll ask Santa for all the expensive toys, ok?"

"Yeah, then you and dad can get us the other stuff!" Emma said.

I felt myself breaking out in a cold sweat as I listened to this conversation unfold. It had quickly taken a turn I wasn't expecting. Before the kids could add swimming pools or trips to Hawaii to their lists, I had to break it to them that Santa has a budget too.

"Mom, guess what? Katie and I are opening up a hair salon today so we can make you look more like a woman." -Ben Hughes

The Magic Show

Emma was fascinated with magic for a few months. She had decided to be a magician and perform onstage in Las Vegas when she turned eight. Of course, this would take a lot of training and practice, of which she did both-constantly. I'm pretty sure I saw about four shows a day during that time.

She had mastered the trick of making Katie and Ben disappear, as long as she had a table and a big blanket handy. But apparently she had learned some new amazing tricks that she was going to debut one afternoon at 3:00 sharp. I popped some popcorn and poured myself a big glass of lemonade to enjoy during the performance.

I sat down to be amazed. She came into the room with a lot of flair, waving her magic wand. "Prepare to be amazed by Emma the magnificent!" She said as she threw some confetti in the air. "My first trick will be to make this dollar bill disappear into thin air," she continued as she stuffed the dollar bill into a cup.

She covered the cup with a paper towel and waved her wand over the top. Then she looked up at me and said, "Now, you have to close your eyes really tight!" Interesting. I just love magic shows where you can't actually see the trick. I shut my eyes tight and when I opened them the money was miraculously gone. *Amazing*.

"For my next trick," she said as she set a glass of water on the table, "I will make this towel change right before your eyes!" She held up one of my dishtowels and then proceeded to dunk it in the water. Then she pulled it out, and let it drip all over the carpet. "Ta-da!" she yelled. "I made it go from dry to wet right before your very eyes!"

"Very impressive," I said as I munched on my popcorn. "I am completely amazed at all of this."

"Do you think I'll be ready for Las Vegas next year?" She asked.

"Not sure about Vegas," I said, "But I'm sure daddy would love to see it tonight."

"Oh man," she moaned, "I thought I was really ready!"

"My only advice is maybe not to ask the audience to close their eyes during a trick- I'm not sure that would go over so well," I told her.

She thought for a minute. "Then how am I supposed to make the money disappear?" She asked. "Just so you know, mom, I don't actually have *real* magic powers."

Whew. Glad she confessed that little secret. I was beginning to wonder, you know.

When You Gotta Go, You Gotta Go

We had the car packed to the brim with sleeping bags, suitcases, beach toys, kites, one dog, three kids and a partridge in a pear tree. Anyway, you get the point. We were cruising down the highway on our way to see family, play at the beach, and hopefully get some much- needed rest. Everyone was happy and the trip had been non-eventful so far. But, as it goes with most of our family vacations, this was to be short lived.

If your family is at all like mine, your kids probably always have to go to the bathroom at *the most inconvenient* times. For example, every single time we go out to eat, one of the kids will have to go poop. It never fails. The minute I start bagging groceries at the store they always have to go. When you're almost to the front of a long line at Disneyland, they have to go. If there's not a toilet in a five-mile radius you can bet money they will need one.

We had already stopped twice for potty breaks during our two- hour drive. We were on the home stretch, only fifteen minutes from our destination. That's when I heard Ben say, "I have to go potty *SO BAD!*" I let out a sigh of frustration as Dave said "You just went thirty minutes ago, can't you hold it?"

Whimpering came from the backseat. Then the panicking started. "It's gonna come out! I can't hold it!" He screamed. There was no place to pull over and hardly any time to think. I quickly scanned the contents of the car and my eyes fell on a Panda Express cup. I grabbed it, took the lid off, and told Ben to pee in it. He had done it before, so he knew the drill.

He hopped down from his seat and I said, "Make sure you aim right into the cup, ok?" I'm still trying to figure out what happened after that. Pee starting flying *everywhere*. Dave took a direct hit to the head, yet still managed to keep his eyes on the road. The front seats and ceiling got sprayed. My arm was completely soaked in a matter of seconds. I let out a scream and dropped the cup. Ben yelled, "I can't stop it, it's coming out too fast!"

Emma yelled at the top of her lungs "What are you doing, Ben?" Unfortunately, this made him turn and spray what was left of his pee ALL OVER HER.

That's when the shrieking began. Emma was mortified. Her right pant leg was soaked, the bottom of her sweatshirt splashed and sadly, oh so sadly, some even got on her hand. This was basically the end of the world to her. She screamed, "Thanks a lot Ben," and then started to sob uncontrollably.

This made Katie cry, who had remained miraculously unscathed. I was frozen in shock and Dave was laughing. Ben crawled back up in his seat and just watched the chaos unfold. Apparently *he* felt a lot better now. Once I got as much cleaned up as I could, and

Emma's sobs got a little quieter, Dave asked, "What were you doing Ben? What happened?"

Ben just shrugged and said, "I started to go and then I think the wind just blew my pee everywhere. Sorry." Even I didn't buy that. "Ben, there's no wind, we're in *THE CAR!*"

He replied, "Well, it's really hard to go potty in a cup when it's so bumpy."

I learned two valuable things from this experience:

1. Don't trust a five- year old to pee in a cup while you're cruising down the highway.

2. If your daughter happens to get peed on by her brother, don't expect her to be ok with it- *EVER.*

Not So Legit

Halfway through Emma's second grade year, we received a letter in the mail from her school. It was to inform us that she had visited the nurse's office fifteen times so far that year. Yes, you read that right- *fifteen times.* I'm sorry, what?

Upon closer inspection, I saw a list of every date and what the complaint was. Some were totally legit and I did vaguely remember her telling me about them. Like the time she fell on the playground and scraped her knee. Or the day she got a bloody nose during class. Or that time she got a paper cut that just needed to have a band aid put on it *right that minute.*

But others were not so legit – she complained of her foot being sore, her shoulder a little itchy, and her ankle feeling funny. But my personal favorite had to be this one- "Your child complained of a stomach ache. While talking to me she passed gas and then said she felt better."

I just love to hear reports about my kids farting in front of other people. It really just makes my day. And don't worry, we were very nice to the school nurse after this incident- she has the patience of a saint, that woman.

"Mommy, Benjamin will NOT let me praise the Lord and its making me so mad!"- Emma Hughes

Entrepreneur

At the ripe age of four years old, Ben purchased his first Velcro wallet at Goodwill for 99 cents. Ever since that day, he has been on a mission to make some cold, hard cash. He started out taking the traditional route: lemonade stands, extra chores, and hunting under couch cushions and car seats.

The problem was that it wasn't adding up very fast. So he decided to try a different tactic. He tried to convince us that there was a book fairy, and that if you left a book under your pillow at night, the book fairy would take it and leave you a quarter. This idea didn't really pan out like he had hoped.

A few weeks later I found him gluing pieces of scrap wood together. He was set on selling his abstract art to all of our neighbors at an event called "Ben's Art Show' (I wasn't embarrassed about this *at all*). He set up his finished pieces out in the driveway, complete with price tags. But before he went door to door handing out flyers, Dave and I ended up buying them all. We told him that we wanted to keep his famous artwork within the family, just in case he was famous one day (I guess this idea did pan out for him- just not for us.).

Eventually he became desperate and actually agreed to pull weeds. But let's face it- that was a lot of work and I'm not sure he felt like he needed the money *that* bad. It's rough to be five and not have a penny to your name.

But the straw came for me one hot summer day. He had spent the whole morning painting beautiful rainbows on white pieces of paper. I thought they were for me and I had grand ideas to frame them and hang them around the house. "Those are beautiful, buddy," I told him, "I can't wait to hang them up!"

"Sorry, mom, these aren't for you," he replied, "I'm going to sell them on Craigslist." Oh. Talk about a major bubble burst. The kid needed an intervention in a bad way. Don't worry- we enrolled him in MMA: moneymakers anonymous. He's doing much better now.

"Mom, when I'm all grown up I will still come and sit on the couch with you and watch whatever movies you want." –Ben Hughes

I Swear to Tell the Truth, the Whole Truth, and nothing but the Truth so Help Me God.

I learned a long time ago that my kids become the best truth-tellers when we're at the Doctor's office. When they're on that exam table, I am completely and utterly helpless as to what will come out of their mouths next. It's kind of like playing with fire; it's only a matter of time before you get burned.

You know those yearly well child questionnaires you have to fill out? About safety, development, diet and TV time? Don't ever fib on those, because your kids will rat you out as soon as you step into that office. Just be truthful from the start- then you might make it out alive.

At Emma's four- year check up I marked that yes, of *course* my child only eats fast food once a week. During our visit her doctor said, "And it looks like you're doing great with fast food, only once a week." Emma looked puzzled, and then she said, "But we eat at McDonalds all the time."

"Okay, just breathe," I thought to myself. I can get through this. Then the Doctor wanted to know what her favorite fruit was. "What's a fruit?" Emma asked her. OH MY WORD. I wanted to crawl under the table and die.

When I took Ben in for his recent check-up she asked him what his favorite thing to do was. "Watch TV," he said very enthusiastically. I could only hang my head in shame. There have been so many other things shared in the confines of that little room, for example:

"My mom lets us skip brushing our teeth sometimes when she's really tired"

"One time we went a whole week without taking our vitamins!"

"I didn't go to sleep until midnight yesterday!"

" I LOVE chicken nuggets."

"My mom forgot to pick me up at school once."

"I don't like to read."

"I actually really like coffee a lot."

I always feel like screaming, "I *do* feed them vegetables! I *do* read to them! And I remember to pick them up from school most of the time. You've got to believe me. I don't know why they're saying these things, but I do limit screen time! Do you see I have *three* of them? They totally outnumber me here!"

But that would make me look even crazier. I'm usually sweating buckets at this point and the room always seems so claustrophobic. Their wonderful doctor just smiles and makes notes in her chart. I think she's reminding herself to pray for me.

At Katie's three- year check-up, I was pleasantly surprised at how well things were going. She sat on the table like a little angel, said her favorite foods were pears and strawberries, and that her favorite thing to do was play outside. I was so happy that for once, no one was throwing mommy under the bus.

Until the very end. "Well, Katie," the Doctor said, "you look great, thanks for coming to see us!"

Katie smiled and then turned to me and said, "I was good, mommy! Now can we go get Icees and French fries at Burger King like you promised?"

We were so close. Maybe next time.

"Mommy, Dance with Kate"

One of the hardest things I've experienced as a parent is to see my child in pain and not be able to make it better. Words can't even describe how this hurts to the core of my very heart and soul. There's a helpless feeling that spreads through every fiber of your being as you watch your baby get wheeled away to surgery- desperately wishing it was you and not them. Watching the clock as the minutes and hours tick away, waiting to hear something-anything.

When Katie was one year old, she got really sick. We assumed it was a bad cold virus, and waited for it to pass. Then she broke out in a rash over her whole body. Her temperature spiked, she wouldn't eat, and she couldn't sleep. We rushed her to the emergency room.

They didn't know what it was. Many doctors and nurses were consulted. A few hours later, the doctor decided to do a strep throat test. He didn't think it would come back positive because of her age, but he wanted to try. It was strep. We were instantly relieved because this was *good* news; it meant she was going to get better.

What we didn't know was this: we would be battling this infection for the next twelve months. That night marked the start of a roller coaster ride of sickness for our family. A year filled with doctor visits, urgent care, sleepless nights and cupboards full of medicine. A year that we couldn't seem to make our baby girl feel better.

Katie got strep five times in ten months. I had to push to get every test done, because the doctors seemed so certain she wouldn't have it again- she was just too little. But she tested positive every time. To make matters worse, the infection was sometimes passed to the rest of us. No one was spared. The final count for strep throat in our family that year was fourteen times. *Fourteen.* The top shelf of our refrigerator was constantly stocked with antibiotics, and sleep became a luxury that we rarely got to enjoy.

About a month after she turned two, Katie got sick *again.* I had just gotten over strep myself, and it was becoming very hard to be positive about anything. I felt like I could never leave the house, my days and nights were all mixed up, and I was so tired that it was hard to even know how to pray anymore.

I took her in to the doctor. The way our insurance worked, if a child got strep throat more than five times in a calendar year, they would approve surgery. I just knew that it would be positive. After all we'd been through, something good had to come of this. She needed surgery. The test needed to be positive.

It was negative. I left the lab in complete and utter shock. We were so close to getting the surgery approved. Why would she be negative now? I cried all the way home. I couldn't imagine another year of seeing her so sick. I missed her smile. I missed her laugh. She needed some relief. I felt panic setting in as I realized her calendar year was up in two months. Then we would be back at square one. I felt helpless.

That night I went for a walk. I cried hard. I kicked at rocks and told God exactly what was on my mind. I was mad, I was frustrated, and I was exhausted. I couldn't believe He wasn't listening to me. I poured out everything that was on my heart, and cried until there was nothing left.

Then, as my anger subsided, an overwhelming peace came over me. I could almost hear these words: "You may not understand right now, but you need to trust me." For the first time in months, I released my control over the situation. I realized I was trying to fix the situation myself, when really I had no control over it at all. I began to pray. But instead of praying for the answer *I wanted*, I prayed that God would give me a sense of peace- peace in *whatever* was supposed to happen.

I turned around and started walking home. That's when my phone rang. It was Katie's doctor. The lab had run a back-up strep test and it was *positive*. The magic number had been reached, and she was already making calls for surgery appointments. I was instantly humbled and amazed at God's grace.

Exactly six days before the year mark of her first strep attack, Dave and I watched them wheel Katie away to surgery. She looked so tiny lying there, and it took all of my self-control not to run after her.

They removed her tonsils and adenoids, and after a couple of days in the hospital, we were heading home. For the first time in a year, I let my body relax. I let myself think about more than just penicillin, throat cultures, body rashes, gagging and late night trips to the ER. God had brought us through a tough time, and I was feeling slivers of hope.

Five days later, I found myself sitting alone on the couch. It was late, and everyone else was already asleep. I knew I should be doing the same- I was so tired. But then I heard a noise coming from down the hall. Pretty soon I saw a cute little wild-haired girl peeking around the corner at me- with a huge mischievous smile on her face. She was supposed to be asleep, but I didn't care. I motioned for her to come, and she did her happy skip run and bounced onto my lap. My heart soared.

"Are you finally feeling better?" I asked her. She smiled and said, "Yep, all better," and she gave me a big hug. The sparkle was returning to her eyes, and I was so happy. We snuggled together and watched Bubble Guppies and Dora the Explorer, we played with Squinkies and Polly Pockets, we ate ice cream straight from the carton and went outside to look at the moon. She reorganized the silverware drawer three times.

At midnight even her cuteness couldn't stop me from getting sleepy. I told her it was time to go to bed. "No mommy," she said as she grabbed my hands, "dance with Kate." I was tired. And I admit that I groaned a little on the inside. But, we turned on a Disney Princess CD and started to dance. We danced fast and we danced slow, we twirled and dipped, and we held on to each other tight. When I spun her around, she giggled until she could hardly breathe. It was the best sound in the whole world.

For our family, it was a season of sickness. A time of not knowing what to do. But for some of you, your life has been turned upside down by childhood illness. Maybe your world has been rocked by these four words - "Your child has cancer." Or maybe they have been battling an ugly disease their whole little life. My heart hurts for you as a write this, because I can't even imagine what it would be like on that journey.

The only thing I know is this: God is listening to our cries. He's listening to our frustration. He's listening even when we're kicking and screaming because we don't think its fair. Sometimes we try so hard to control everything, when all He wants is for us to release it to him-to take a deep breath, and put our faith and trust in Him and His plan for our lives.

When we watch our baby roll through those double doors into surgery, God knows exactly how we feel. When we hold our crying child in our arms and we can't make them feel better, He knows exactly how we feel. When we can't bear to see our loved ones suffering, He knows exactly how we feel. After all, He gave His one and only Son to save *me*- to save *all of us*. Jesus was beaten, ridiculed and nailed to a cross. He suffered, died, and rose again so that we may live in eternity with Him. God understands how it feels to see your child suffer.

It's really hard to let go of control. But believe me, God is doing great works even through the raging storms in our lives. He has a purpose for them, and even though we may not understand, He is always there. Lean on Him when you can't go another step by yourself. He will never leave your side.

Nails like a Witch

As I was finishing up my 2.5 minute shower at 11:00am (you heard me right), I heard a blood-curdling scream. I was sure it was Katie and that I would soon be headed to the ER in nothing but a towel. The bathroom door flew open and there was Ben, holding his finger like it had been cut off right at the knuckle.

I feared the worst and quickly stepped out of the shower, dripping wet with soap still in my hair. The sobs were uncontrollable. "What's wrong?" I yelled above all the hysteria. I braced myself as I pulled his hand away. All I could make out was a little *tiny* dot of blood.

He caught his breath just long enough to whimper, "Katie scratched me with her huge giant claw!" I glanced up and there was Kate peaking around the corner with apparently ten razor- sharp fingernails. I'm not sure it's possible to be more dramatic. As I put a Band-Aid over the small scratch, I gently reminded him that his little sister is all of two feet tall and *maybe* thirty pounds. "But she has nails like a witch!" He protested. I sighed and told him to go play.

That night I did trim her freakishly long nails. And if you're wondering, I never did get to finish my shower-leftover soap residue is really in right now.

"Mom, it's really hard being so popular all the time."- Ben Hughes

Fashionista

I was frantically packing up lunches when I remembered that it was a PE day for Emma at school. "Don't forget to wear your socks and tennis shoes today!" I yelled down the hall to her.

"I'm just going to take them in my backpack because I want to look pretty!" She yelled back.

I was in too big of a hurry to argue. A few minutes later we were pulling up to the school and saying goodbye. As she walked through the double doors my eyes zeroed in on her feet. Interesting. She was wearing her black high heels. The only problem was that she had paired them with her *huge* Nike athletic socks. Lord have mercy.

Sherlock Holmes

The afternoon had been chalk-full of errands, grocery shopping and very whiney kids. As we trudged into the empty house, I heard a strange noise coming from the hall bathroom. It sounded like water running. I set the milk down and went to investigate. Sure enough, the water in the sink had been running full blast- the entire time we were gone.

"I need everybody in here right now!" I yelled. The sound of little feet running down the hallway followed. There they stood in front of me- all three of them. "What's wrong, mom?" Emma asked.

"Who left the water running after they washed their hands?" I asked with my hands on my hips. Awkward silence followed. No one moved except for Katie, who was shaking her head yes, then no, and then yes again. No one made eye contact, lest they should draw more attention to themselves.

Finally, Ben broke through the tension-filled air and said, "Well, I think I can solve this mystery." He tapped his finger to his chin and thought for a few seconds. "Katie can't even reach the sink," he continued, "so it for sure wasn't her. And Emma always turns it off." Suddenly his eyes got as big as saucers. "Oh, man, I guess that means it was me."

I love it when my kids incriminate themselves accidentally. It sure saves me a lot of time and energy.

Smart Aleck

I was at the end of my rope. The night was quickly going from bad to worse and I was trying to get kids into bed. My patience was running thin as I barked out orders over the chaos: "Brush your teeth! Clean up those toys! Finish your homework!"

I heard a loud noise coming from Ben's room so I went to investigate. He was throwing toys into his drawers from across the room. I took a deep breath and said, "How about we try and be a little quieter!"

He looked at me and said, "How about we try and not be so bossy?"

Me: "Kate, you need to go brush your teeth."

Kate: "No thanks, I'm pretty bored of doing that."

The Game that shall not be named

My kids have a game they like to play when they're bored. It's called 'Raise your hand if…' The game usually takes place in the car, but really it can be played anywhere: at the dinner table, around the campfire, sitting in the waiting room, and while trying to go to sleep.

Someone will start the game and ask a question like, "Raise your hand if you like to swim with sharks!" Then you make the excruciating decision as to whether or not to raise your hand. It's a tough call sometimes.

One day as I was folding laundry, the kids and I were playing this very game. Lots of fun questions had been asked, ranging from "Raise your hand if you like spiders" to "Raise your hand if you like to eat boogers." We were all laughing.

When it was Katie's turn she said, "Raise your hand if you like to eat." They all raised their hands and then Emma looked at me and said, "You better raise your hand really high on this one mom- you love to eat". Thanks. Thanks a lot. The game was then banned from our house until I could regain some of my self-esteem back.

My Favorite Thing All Summer

The summer was quickly coming to an end. But before we put the tent away, Dave and Ben wanted to have one more camp-out in the backyard. The girls and I on the other hand, preferred the comfort of our own beds. We'd already spent many cold nights in the great outdoors, and didn't feel the need to do it *again*.

But I still wanted to make the night special for them. I let them choose a movie, we painted our nails, and roasted s'mores over the stove. Katie crashed out around 10 o'clock, but Emma and I stayed up playing Barbie's until 11:30. We had a blast.

A few days later, I was sitting on the edge of Emma's bed saying goodnight. The next day was the start of a brand-new school year. I asked her, "So, what was your all-time favorite thing we did ALL summer?"

As she thought about it, my thoughts drifted back over the last two and a half months. We had packed a lot in: camping trips, museums, swimming lessons, bike rides, trips to see family, sleepovers, vacations and lots of friends. She looked at me with a big smile on her face and said, "Playing Barbie's with you all by myself for two whole hours. That was my absolute favorite thing all summer!" I couldn't believe it. She really thought that was better than our fun vacations?

Later, as I lay in bed, I realized what the difference had been. She loved doing all the other things too, but this was her favorite because it made her feel special. She knew I was choosing to spend my night playing with her, no distractions getting in our way. I was truly focused on *her*; I listened to her, laughed with her, and was silly with her. And that made her very happy.

Doesn't God desire that with us? To truly have our undivided attention with no distractions? He delights in our company, He wants a relationship with us, and He wants us to choose *Him*. So often we push Him aside because we're just too busy. All of those vacations we took as a family were fun, but they were *busy*. We were together, but we were rushing. It was very hard to get any one- on- one time with each other.

But sometimes that's exactly what we need. Emma was craving time with just me. She wanted me to be in the moment with her, focusing on her, strengthening our relationship. She wanted to feel special, set apart, and loved.

I desperately need that. We all do. I want to set aside distractions and choose time with my Savior. I need

Him, and when I get too busy, I know something is missing. I crave time to just be with Him- to feel loved and special. And just like Emma said to me that night, I want to be able to say, "My favorite part of the day was being in the presence of the Lord."

Denial

I had been outside doing yard work and came in to get a drink. I heard a movie playing in the family room so I went to check it out. There was Ben, sitting in front of the television, watching Barbie in the Mermaid Kingdom. *Alone.* I could hear Katie playing in her room.

I cleared my throat. He whipped around and froze like a deer caught in the headlights. "I was *NOT* watching this," he said shaking his head.

"Sure looks like you were," I smiled, "It's a good movie, huh?"

"I don't know if it's good, I wasn't watching it, remember?" He stated uncomfortably.

"You were staring right at the screen," I said.

"Well, I came in here to get my army guys," he explained, "but then I tripped right in front of the TV. I guess I was just resting until my knee felt better."

"Well, just so you know, it's fine to watch a Barbie movie every now and then," I said. "Someday your wife will be really happy you can sit through movies like this."

"Now you're just talking crazy," he said as he stomped out of the room. I decided to leave the movie playing, just in case he 'tripped' again before it was over.

Give the Lady What She Wants

Around 3:00am I was jolted awake by a little hand rubbing my face. I couldn't see much in the dark but I could hear whimpering. It was Katie. "What's wrong," I whispered sleepily.

"You didn't put my right jammies on," she said and then broke out into uncontrollable sobs. I had no idea what she was talking about. But I knew I didn't want her to wake up the entire house, either.

I quickly walked her back to her room. In the glow of the nightlight, I saw that she had on her pink flower pajamas. She began pulling and tugging at them. "What are you doing?" I whisper-yelled. In between sobs she yelled out, "These jammies are not my favorite. You promised me Ariel jammies!"

I stared at her. And then something jogged my memory. This morning after breakfast she had asked me to wash her Ariel pajamas so she could wear them again. I had promised her I would. But the day had been busy, and her special pajamas sat unwashed at the bottom of the hamper.

"Let's just wear these for the rest of the night and then mommy will wash the Ariel ones tomorrow, ok?" I said as I tried to put her back in bed. She went limp-boneless. She wouldn't move and wouldn't cooperate. My two-year old was quickly sending me into a panic-attack. I had to get a hold of the situation.

I left her crying on the floor of her room. I ran down the hall and flipped on the laundry room light. I dug through that hamper like my life depended on it. Clothes were flying in every direction as I frantically continued my search. And then, there they were, underneath a dirty baseball uniform. I grabbed them, held them tight to my chest, and I think I even kissed them- I'm not sure, it's all such a blur.

I hurried back down the hall and prayed to God this would work. I was so tired. The minute she saw those pajamas her sobs turned into shouts of joy. She hugged them and said "Tank you, mommy, tank you SO much," as she wiped away her tears. They were covered in maple syrup, peanut butter, and ketchup- but she didn't care. I snuggled her up with blankets and she was fast asleep before I even left the room. I stumbled back to my bed in a daze. I felt like I had just lived out a scene of a horror movie.

I am now much more cautious about making promises. The wrath of a two-year old in the dead of night can really scare some sense into you.

"Dear Lord, thank you for this day, and please help us to get full on pizza because apparently that's all we're having. Amen."- Emma Hughes

The Man on the Corner

Ben and I were in the car, busy running errands and playing the animal thinking game. I was so close to guessing what his secret animal was. We pulled up to a stoplight and I asked, "Does it live in a tree?" He didn't answer me. "Hello back there," I said, "Are you listening?"

"Be quiet a minute, mom," he said, "I need to pray for that man over there. He doesn't have a leg." I scanned the intersection and my eyes fell on a man sitting in his wheelchair. His right leg was gone and grocery bags hung from the handles of his chair. I was humbled right away and I said, "Ok, go ahead."

His prayer went like this: "Jesus, help that man not to be sad. Help him to have friends and be happy. Help him to grow a new leg or get money for a fake leg. Amen." A few seconds of silence followed. In the rearview mirror I could see big crocodile tears welling up in his eyes as he watched the man cross in front of us.

"That was nice, buddy," I said.

He sat there watching the man slowly move down the street. "I hope I could be that brave," he whispered quietly.

The light turned green and just like that the moment was over. He went back to playing the game, and acting silly. But suddenly every little thing I had been worried about faded away. I blinked hot tears away and smiled at the boy sitting in the backseat. He was not too busy to notice that man. He wasn't too busy to stop and pray.

God uses our kids in amazing ways. They help us see the world in a different light. They help us slow down and realize what's important. That night I prayed that God would help me slow down, look outside of myself and notice the people around me. To give me the heart of a child, and take time to pray every chance I get. And mostly, I prayed, help me not miss these moments because I am just too busy to listen.

That Kind of Morning

It was early in the morning and I was just brewing myself a cup of coffee. Katie came stumbling into the kitchen with her blanket in tow. Her wild hair was sticking straight up and her eyes were squinting from the bright lights of the kitchen.

"Well, good morning," I said as I scooped her up for a hug. She grabbed my face with her little hands. "I'm hungry," she muttered.

"What, no cuddles for mommy this morning?" I replied. She shook her head no. "Ok," I said as I set her down, "I think we've got oatmeal, cereal, strawberries, yogurt and eggs. What do you want?"

She thought about it for a minute and then whispered, "I'll just have some M&M's. And maybe some marshmallows." I stared at her. She stared back at me. It was a stand off just like those of the Wild West.

I decided to stand my ground. "Sorry, that's not even an option," I told her. She frowned and stomped her way over to the couch to lay down. It was in that moment that I realized it would be a two-cups of coffee kind of morning.

Slug Bug Game

Nothing good ever comes from the slug bug game. If you think that's a false statement then you are in serious denial. My sisters and I fought over this very game for almost two decades. I'm pretty sure we used it as an excuse to punch each other without the threat of getting in trouble. Most of the time, though, the game turned ugly and we would find ourselves sitting in stony silence for the rest of the car ride.

Unfortunately, my kids have carried on this tradition wholeheartedly. When they were little, the game was harmless and fun. One of them would yell, "Slug bug green!" and everyone would clap. It was this perfect little world where everyone got along and cheered for each other.

Then they grew up. They got competitive and embraced the idea of punching each other. I was forced to lay down some ground rules, one of which included not hitting *hard*. It had to be more of a love pat. This did not work at all.

One day as we drove home from church, they started playing the slug bug game. By the fourth slug bug citing, tempers were flaring and many tears had already been shed. I had reached the end of my rope with this game. I yelled in my scariest mommy voice, "NO MORE SLUG BUG GAME- EVER! It is banned from this car!"

Five seconds of uncomfortable silence followed. Then Emma mumbled, "That's not fair."

"It is fair!" I said loudly. "It's totally fair because *no one* will be allowed to play, understand? The next person that yells out slug bug is going on time-out when we get home!"

The next couple of miles passed by in peace and quiet. Then suddenly Emma yelled, "Mom, Ben is smiling every time a slug bug goes by! He's totally playing the game in his head! Can he do that? That's not fair, right?"

I couldn't believe what I was hearing. I glanced back and Ben shrugged his shoulders with a big smile pasted on his face. Even in silence the slug bug game was ruining my day. I may never be totally rid of it.

Me: "Why is Katie crying?"

Ben: "I gave her a hug- that's all I know."

Me: "Why would she be crying if you gave her a hug?"

Ben: "Well, I did hit her *before* I gave her the hug, so I think maybe that's the real reason she's crying."

Mt. Everest

Occasionally our family gets a little behind on laundry. And by a little I mean we pretty much have nothing left to wear that's not covered in food or snot. When no one can find a pair of clean underwear to save their life, I buckle down and do some laundry.

I'm really good at getting loads of laundry into the washer and dryer. It's the folding part that is just AWFUL. Some people like to fold clothes- they find it somewhat therapeutic. I find that it gives me extreme heartburn and makes me nauseous. God is obviously still working on my attitude in this area of my life.

One particular winter, the situation got very bad. I could blame it on any number of things, but I won't. It started innocently with one clean load of laundry dumped in the corner of our bedroom. I was late for a PTA meeting, and I told myself I would fold the pile that night when the kids went to bed. No harm in that, right?

Two weeks and twenty loads later that little pile became a gigantic mountain. I could barely get by it to crawl into bed at night. The kids began referring to it as Mt. Everest. Dave simply called it the giant pile. "Hey Nik, I actually found a matching pair of socks in the giant pile this morning," he would say with excitement, like it was some huge feat he had accomplished.

At first we all joked about it. We laughed at how big it had gotten and what people would think if they opened the door to our bedroom. But then something scary happened. The mountain of clothes actually became a part of our house. A permanent fixture that no one even questioned anymore. We didn't even joke about it. It was just a fact of life.

Instead of knowing which drawers our clothes were in, we knew where they were in the pile. One day Emma yelled from her room, "Mom, where are my basketball shorts?" I yelled right back, "On the right side of Mt. Everest, about half-way down near the wall." A few seconds later she responded, "Got it. Thanks."

Ben came up to me one morning and told me he had no clean underwear. Before I had the chance to answer he said, "Oh, I forgot to look on Mt. Everest." It was sad, really. Or maybe it wasn't? I had almost convinced myself that we had stumbled upon a better and more fluent system for doing laundry. I was obviously in extreme denial.

I was snapped back to reality the night the kids and I played hide and seek. When one of your kids can successfully win this game by hiding inside your mountain of laundry, it's time for it to go. Or when your two-year old says that her favorite part of the day was climbing Mt. Everest all by herself, it's time to let it go.

It took me four excruciating hours to remove Mt. Everest. The only thing that kept me going during those dark hours was this thought: "Nikki, when you wake up in the middle of the night to pee, you won't have to crawl over the clothes to get to the bathroom!"

I vowed to myself that very day that I would change my ways. I would fold the clothes as soon as they came out of the dryer. I would keep on top of the laundry instead of it on top of me. I was determined to never let Mt. Everest reappear in our house. And it didn't- for at least three entire weeks.

The Egg Juggler

One of Emma and Ben's daily chores is to get the chicken eggs out of the nesting box. They trade off weeks, and after a few rotations I began to notice something very strange. When it was Emma's week to get the eggs, we would have 12-14 of them by Saturday. But when it was Ben's week, the egg carton still sat half-empty by the weekend. Something very suspicious was going on between the chicken coop and the kitchen door.

So, one morning I decided to send Emma with him to collect the eggs. A few minutes later they came back, and Ben only had one egg in his hand.

"What is going on with the eggs?" I asked him. He shrugged and mumbled something as he walked over to the refrigerator.

I turned to Emma, who looked like she had some very juicy information to share with me. "What's going on?" I asked her.

Emma said, "Ben dropped two eggs on the way back to the house- he was juggling with them!"

I turned and stared at him. "Seriously?" I said. "Ben, we have to be careful with the eggs, that's why we have chickens in the first place!"

"I am careful," he said with determination.

Then Emma said, "No you weren't, you were throwing them up in the air and catching them!"

Ben looked at me and said, "Well, I try to be careful when I throw them up in the air- but the catching part is really hard."

Ben: "Mommy, is doing something on purpose mean I have to go on time- out?"

Me: "Yes."

Ben: "OK, I hit Emma on accident then."

She's Already There

I'm eight years old and I can't breathe. I wake up in a panic and covered in sweat. It takes all my energy to just suck in a little bit of air. My chest heaves with the effort. I don't remember calling out her name, but she's already there. She knew I needed her. She's already setting up my breathing machine and whispering for me to relax, to calm down.

She's rubbing my head with a wet washcloth and saying calmly, "If you panic, it will only get worse." She pulls me onto her lap and starts to breathe deep, over and over again. My body starts to relax and I release my grip on the sheets. My body becomes in tune with hers. I can feel the up and down motion of her chest and the fear starts to leave me. "That's it," she says quietly, "that's much better."

I still can't talk and my mouth and lips are dry from trying to get air. She puts the mask on me and starts up the machine. The medicine slowly fills my lungs and relief floods my body. I start to shake and feel lightheaded. She says, "Now breath slowly, not too fast." She rubs my back and sings to me.

She carries me downstairs and we sit on the couch together. It's three in the morning, but she turns on Winnie the Pooh and we watch it together. I drift off to sleep for awhile and when I wake up she's still there. She's watching me breathe. She's still rubbing my back and whispering prayers that I will be better.

I finally fall into a deep sleep because I know she will stay with me. I know she will take care of me. And I know that she loves me with every fiber of her being. I feel safe. And I feel lucky. And I know that's the kind of mom I want to be someday.

Mystery Solved

We were cruising down the highway when I suddenly heard a gasp from the backseat. "Mommy," Katie said in a panicked voice, "I have a new nipple growing on my arm!"

This brought roars of laughter from Emma and Ben. "It's not funny!" Katie yelled at them. "It's a big new nipple- see Mommy!"

"I'm driving, Kate. I can't see it. Show Emma," I said.

"I don't want any nipples on my arm," Kate said nervously as she held her arm out towards Emma.

"Those are called FRECKLES Katie, not nipples," Emma said laughing hysterically.

"Oh, I have a new freckle growing on my arm, mommy," Katie said.

"Thank goodness," I said seriously.

"Yeah," she replied.

"I can't believe Kate thought a boob was growing on her arm," Ben said with a huge smile.

"Alright, we solved the mystery," I tried to say with a straight face. "Now let's stop having this really weird conversation, ok?"

Hidden Agenda

Ben wanted to help me make dinner. When someone in my family offers to lend a hand, I have a very hard time refusing. I can use all the help I can get. So I told him that was fine, and he could be in charge of the salad.

He pulled the lettuce, carrots and cucumbers out of the refrigerator. Then he headed out to the garden to find the rest of his ingredients. A few minutes later he was busy rinsing off snap peas, tomatoes and strawberries in the sink. He seemed very happy and willing to do whatever was needed.

I helped him chop everything up, and then he carefully divided the salad into five different bowls. He was unusually quiet during this whole process. About ten minutes later I said, "Ben, dinner's ready so go ahead and put the salad's on the table."

He quickly replied, "That's ok, mom, I'll just keep them here on the counter for a little while."

"How come?" I asked.

"Well, I'm actually charging for these salads," he said very seriously, "I don't want everybody to start eating them before they pay me."

"So, we have to pay to eat the salad you made?" I asked.

"It's just a dollar per salad," he said, "that's a really good deal."

I just love being charged for food that I already paid for once.

A Little on Edge

Katie was taking a shower while I put on my make-up. I said, "Hey, I'm going to go grab you a towel from the other bathroom, ok?"

"Ok, mom," she yelled back. I was gone exactly eight seconds. When I came back I opened up the shower curtain to wash her hair. She looked absolutely scared out of her mind and she threw the shampoo bottle at me.

"What on earth is wrong?" I asked her. She let out a sigh of relief and with a nervous giggle she said, "I thought you were a stranger!"

Car Insurance

One rainy afternoon, the kids made up a game called "pass the toy around." Basically, it was like hot potato; you passed the toy around the circle until the music stopped. But in their version, the person holding the toy would win a prize. For the game, Ben had ransacked his room to come up with a box of prizes to give out.

Emma and Katie had won almost all the rounds, and gotten a lot of cool prizes. FINALLY the toy landed with me. I could hardly contain my excitement. Ben carried the bucket over to me and said, "Sorry, mom, it looks like the only prizes left are a flyer to do gymnastics and a coupon to save money on car insurance."

I hung my head. "Well, it's a little late in my life to start a career in gymnastics," I said, "so I guess I'll take the car insurance coupon."

"Why do you have a coupon in your room for car insurance?" Emma asked.

My thoughts exactly.

"God is great, God is good, thank you God for our food, and please help Jesus to be good up there. Amen"- Emma Hughes

Lost and Found

I broke the news to the kids at 10:30 on a Saturday morning. I had waited until they had a chance to sleep in, catch a couple cartoons, eat breakfast and do some coloring. But then I just *had* to tell them. I wasn't happy about it, but I said the dreaded words- "you three have got to clean your rooms. They are seriously DISGUSTING."

Three smiles instantly turned to frowns; three happy voices were suddenly silenced. Sometimes the truth hurts.

"But mom, it's *Saturday*," Emma whined.

"Nope, I don't want to hear it," I said, "the fun stuff has to wait until the rooms are clean."

Dejected, they headed down the hall. About ten minutes later Ben yelled from his room, "I'm done, mom!" I thought that seemed pretty fast, given that I could hardly see the carpet this morning. So I went to inspect. Much to my surprise, every inch of the floor was clean and the shelves were neat and tidy. I was shocked.

Then I noticed the sheet hanging from his top bunk. Apparently he had also found time to build a fort underneath his bed. "So, what's going on in there," I said pointing towards his bunk bed.

"Oh, don't worry about that," he said as he moved to stand in front of it.

"I think I'll just take a quick peep," I said cautiously. I lifted the sheet and there, piled high on the bottom mattress, was *everything* that had been on the floor.

I turned and stared him down. Without blinking an eye he said, "Oh, that? That's just my lost and found area."

"So basically you moved all the stuff from the floor to your new 'lost and found' area?" I asked.

"It's a lot easier this way, mom," he said. "Next time just don't look under the sheet, ok?"

Simplicity

Have you ever longed for simplicity? Not just as an afterthought, I'm talking about for *real.* The true gut-wrenching need that starts deep down in your soul and wrestles itself to the surface: the need for stillness, quiet, time, and peace. With the amount of technology at our fingertips, the fast pace of life, and the pressure to be everything to everyone all the time, it's hard to just be still. Sometimes I lie awake at night just staring into the darkness. How can I possibly keep up with everything? How can I do it all? Why is this so hard? I find myself saying these words over and over again in my head: *there has to be a better way.*

I was in the car pick-up line at Emma and Ben's school waiting for the throes of kids to come out the double doors. Usually I'm busy trying to entertain Katie while we wait, but on this day she had fallen asleep. It gave me time to look around. I was amazed at the number of parents glued to their iPhones. Talking on them, texting, playing games and adding dates to their calendars. Now, I'm not against ANY of these things; I have a cell phone too and use it quite regularly. But what my eyes were opened to for the first time was this: Most parents didn't even look up when their kids ran up to them. I saw kid after kid walk up to their parent and get shushed, ignored, or just simply told to get in the car.

They never put down the phone. I felt humbled instantly. Have we become SO connected to the world of technology that we are *missing* what's right in front of us? Are we losing touch with what's real? Do we really want our kids to think that the ring of a cell phone trumps them telling us about their day? Do we want our spouse to think we care more about chatting on facebook than actually talking to them? Do we want our kids to remember us sending text after text instead of pushing them on the swings at the park? We've become disconnected, and I don't like it- *at all.*

One night I had simply had enough. Things just seemed to be spiraling out of control. It had not been a good day. There's just no better way to put it. The craziness of the evening was in full motion. I was trying to get the kitchen cleaned up from dinner. There was a lot of whining going on: toys that needed batteries, cuts that needed band-aids, dolls that needed that one special dress *right this minute.* The news was on in the kitchen, Just Dance Kids was blaring "Kung Fu Fighting" from the other room, Dave's work phone was going off, and my cell said I had 3 new text messages.

I started crying. All of the sudden it was too much. I couldn't even think straight. I wanted to SMASH every piece of technology we owned. And then I had a revelation: there *IS* a better way. It was a moment of clarity that I totally believe was the Holy Spirit. A peace fell over me and I set the rag down right in the middle of scrubbing the counters. *Go outside.* That's what I needed to do. I left the kitchen, grabbed a blanket and walked straight out the front door.

I laid out my blanket in the middle of the front yard and stared up at the sky- *peace.* I felt it instantly- a new perspective. I laid out there alone for only a few minutes. I knew they would come. Emma was the first to come out. She lay down by me and asked, "What are you doing out here?"

"Looking up in the sky," I said. She looked up and as if on cue, a falling star shot right in front of us! She screamed and that brought out Ben. He plopped down next to me and snuggled his head into my neck. A few minutes later I heard the TV's turn off inside, the porch lights went dark, and Dave and Katie came out to join us.

It wasn't quiet anymore but we were together. We were talking with no distractions. It wasn't complicated. It felt right. It felt like *the better way.* I know we will probably relapse and fall into old patterns. But I am earnestly praying that we all can live in the moment. That God will stir in us a desire to prioritize what is important. Hug your kids. Grab their little faces smeared with jelly and tell them how much you love them. Put down your phone when your man walks through the door. Be there for each other and listen. Turn off the distractions and *talk to each other.*

God has a lot to teach us if we will just stop for a minute and listen. Believe me, life will go on if you don't answer every single text. Life will go on if you don't check facebook every single day. Life will go on if you choose to read books with your four- year old instead of answering the phone. Try to prioritize what's important. There is a better way.

Trouble with Technology

Katie wanted to watch a movie so I brought up Netflix on our TV. She was sitting comfortably on the couch as it loaded. When I finally got to the Netflix kids screen, I asked her what she wanted to watch. I patiently waited while she looked at the screen. Then, she got up and walked over to the TV. She proceeded to try and swipe the rows of movies to the left and right with her finger.

"Hey!" she yelled in frustration. "Why is this not working!" She tried to swipe at the screen some more. "It's frozen mommy!"

I stood behind her holding the remote in disbelief. I had to break it to her that there are still certain appliances that don't have touch-screen capabilities.

In an Instant

My alarm clock went off at six that morning, and I could see rays of sunlight peaking through the shades. I hadn't slept much the night before; I was too excited about what the following day would bring. I was going to get an ultrasound of our little baby. I was so excited to see this brand new miracle growing inside of me.

I left the house quietly, my family still sound asleep. I couldn't wait to bring home a picture to show Emma and Ben. In the weeks since we had told Emma the wonderful news, she had named our baby Rose. She seemed pretty certain that God was going to give her a sister. We were all very excited, and as I drove to the doctor's office that glorious spring day, I felt truly blessed.

In the waiting room, I absently flipped through magazines. But mostly I was lost in my own thoughts. I was surprised by how much I was looking forward to this moment. This was my third pregnancy, and I just assumed that these 'firsts' would lose their luster. But that was so far from the truth. Just like with my other two precious kids, I was overcome with love for that baby already. I couldn't stop smiling.

"Mrs. Hughes," they called, "we're ready for you." I walked back and undressed in a small dark room. I situated myself on the exam table, and waited for the ultrasound tech to come in. The room was cold and suddenly I felt very alone. I was regretting not having Dave there with me. He had been there for every other ultrasound, but life was a lot busier now. Since it was such an early appointment, we had decided he should stay home.

"Good morning," said the technician, "let's get started." She lubed up my belly with the gel that they pull straight out of the freezer. She turned the machine on, and then adjusted the screen so that I could see. "OK," she said, "Here we go."

I heard the familiar sound of static as she rubbed around all over my belly. My head was propped up in anticipation as she zeroed in on the amniotic sac. Then she quit talking. She zoomed in and stared hard at the screen. I suddenly couldn't breathe. I felt like the air had been sucked right out of the room. I had done this too many other times to deny what I was seeing. I didn't see the little heart beating, there was no movement, there was no sound coming from the machine.

I stared at that monitor just begging for it all to be a bad dream. "I'm sorry," she said, "but it looks as if you've had a miscarriage." I heard her words, but they sounded like they were coming from the end of a long tunnel. I felt completely numb and empty.

"What?" I asked with my voice shaking and tears running down my face. "Please look again, there's got to be a mistake!" She stared at the screen a few seconds longer, and then quietly shut it off. She wiped off the gel as I let my tears flow.

"Your doctor will be in touch in the next few days. You can get dressed now." And then I was alone. In exactly nine minutes my life had been turned upside down. I was shaking so bad I could hardly get my clothes back on. I don't even remember walking out of the office building. But I do remember climbing behind the wheel, closing the door, and sobbing until I had nothing left in me.

It was 7:45 when I pulled into our driveway. The house was exactly as I had left it, but so much had changed. I let the dog out, I turned the coffee on, and I opened the shades. I silently walked down our hallway- everyone was still asleep. As I opened the door to our bedroom, the tears started falling again. I climbed into bed with my coat and shoes still on. I got as close to Dave as I could and cried my eyes out.

He held me for a long time, unsure of what to say. He had no idea what was wrong. I couldn't find the words to tell him- and I didn't want to. Finally, I couldn't cry anymore. "We lost the baby," I whispered.

He pulled me even closer and silently let his tears fall. When the kids woke up a few minutes later, we pulled them into bed with us- suddenly much more aware of the fragility of life, of the things that are most important to us, and of how quickly life can change.

Good List and Bad List

One morning Katie crawled up into my lap and looked right into my eyes. She grabbed my cheeks and said, "Mommy, I love you." My heart melted and I gave her a huge hug. Then she added this little gem: "And I wanted you to know you're on my good list today."

"What do you mean, I'm on your good list?" I asked.

"You just are. You're on my good list right now," she said.

"Am I sometimes not on your good list?" I asked with apprehension.

"Yes," she said seriously, "some days you're on a bad list."

Then she ran away to laugh and frolic in the yard. It was scary.

Three- year olds often remind me of high profile mobsters like Al Capone and Bugs Moran. And here's why I think that:

1. They are very powerful (but in a highly illegal sort of way).

2. They are willing to go to extreme measures to get what they want.

3. They have high profile connections to accomplish what's important to them (dad, grandma, grandpa, aunts, and uncles.).

4. They can be borderline bi-polar and easily set off.

5. They instill fear in those that dare to cross them, or God forbid tell them *NO*.

6. They are extremely crafty.

7. They have good lists and bad lists. Enough said.

So try and stay on Katie's good list if you ever cross her path- who knows what she's planning next.

Thistle in my Pants

When you're dealing with kids, you know that anything can happen at any given moment. I was very naïve about this particular fact before I had kids. Every single kid should come with a disclaimer that reads ATTENTION: THIS KID WILL TELL EVERY ONE OF YOUR SECRETS AT THE MOST INAPPROPRIATE TIMES. SHE WILL THROW UP ON YOU EVERY TIME YOU ARE ABOUT TO LEAVE THE HOUSE. HE WILL POOP EVERY SINGLE TIME YOU FORGET TO

BRING A DIAPER BAG. THIS KID WILL EAT GUM FROM UNDERNEATH RESTAURANT TABLES. SHE WILL STRIP DOWN NAKED WHEN YOU HAVE COMPANY OVER FOR NO GOOD REASON. HE WILL RAT YOU OUT EVERY TIME YOU DRIVE AND TALK ON THE PHONE. THIS KID WILL NEVER LET YOU SLEEP AGAIN.

You get the point, right? It's an adventure just to get up in the morning, because I literally have no idea how my day will pan out. For example, one early summer morning I decided to take the kids strawberry picking. We spent a fun couple of hours picking strawberries- well, I should say that *some* of us picked them. Katie did a lot of eating. She would pick one, then eat one. Pick one, then eat one.

We really had a great time. Not wanting the fun to end, we headed to meet some friends for a play date to get even more energy out. Things were going so great and everyone was happy.

We were a little early so I pulled into a grocery store parking lot to kill some time. As I parked the car Ben started complaining about his pants itching. He unbuckled his seatbelt and started hopping around. "I think there's a thistle in my pants!" He yelled. Before I could even say anything he was stripping down. His pants flew off. Shirt next. Then socks. He was shaking his jeans out like his life depended on it.

I said, "Give me the pants so I can check them for you." He stopped scratching just long enough to toss me the pants. He's not dramatic or anything.

I inspected them and found nothing. Zip. Nada. But he was still dancing like a wild man and then he yelled out, "I think it's in my underwear!" You guessed it- off came the underwear.

Now, here's where it got interesting. The girls had been buckled in this whole time, watching the scenario unfold. Katie's car seat was next to Ben, so unfortunately she was strapped in with a close up view of this spontaneous strip show. When the underwear flew off, she let out a gagging sound- a GAGGING sound. But I was still sidetracked trying to find the HUGE thistle that I didn't pay close attention.

Apparently the sight of her brothers naked rear end was enough to send her stomach into convulsions. The gagging got worse. I dropped the underwear and flipped around in my seat. "Honey, what's wrong?" I asked.

She pointed at Ben and said, "His butt is grossing me…." Just then she was interrupted by another gagging episode. I jumped out of the car and unbuckled her as fast as I could. The minute I pulled her out, up came *every single* strawberry she secretly ate at the farm, along with her whole lunch.

It was only after she finished throwing up that I realized I had left the back door open. I'm sure the grocery store patrons really appreciated seeing a naked kid inside a car watching his sister throw up in the parking lot. I'm surprised someone didn't call the heat on me.

I threw Ben's underwear back at him as Katie climbed back into her seat. As she sat down she said, "Don't you ever show your butt at me again Ben."

It all happened very fast. But I will tell you that no thistle or anything closely resembling a thistle was ever found in his pants or underwear. I'm telling you, kids don't come with enough disclaimers.

Emma: "Mom, was daddy born in the olden days?"

Me: "What do you mean by the olden days?"

Emma: "Like before iPhones. You know, when there were those booths you had to put money in to call somebody on the side of the road."

The Silverware Drawer

For some time now I have been flabbergasted as to why my silverware drawer is always sticky. I clean it and then a couple days later it's gross again. Little piles of stickiness and crumbs creep their way onto the spoons, knives and forks. Complaining about it to the kids has done no good; they just look at me with a sad expression like they think I belong in a mental institution.

But then I solved the mystery- I watched firsthand as Emma got a spoon out of the drawer, poured herself some milk, added chocolate and gave the milk a nice long swirl. Then, she promptly put the spoon right back in the drawer. I was standing right there! She was chatting with me the whole time like this was TOTALLY normal.

"What are you doing?" I yelled with my eyes bulging out a little.

"What?" she asked as she set her glass down.

"Get that dirty spoon out of the silverware drawer!" I said.

"Ok, Ok, I'm getting it," she said. "It's gonna be ok, mom, it's just a spoon."

I stood there staring at her. It was about WAY more than the spoon, and I was trying to decide what to say first. She must have finally picked up on the tension that filled the air, because she quickly said, "Oh, we have to wash the spoon first, right? I'll just do that right now and then I'll get out of your way. You can have some quiet time."

I watched as she set it in the sink and then backed out of the kitchen. Then she ran away. I guess after ten years, I have finally mastered the mind melding capabilities of a seasoned mom. No one can stop me now.

I Love You More than Thunder Eggs and Sand Dollars

One night as I was tucking Ben into bed, he suddenly wrapped his arms around my neck and said, "Mom, I love you more than thunder eggs and sand dollars."

"Thanks, buddy," I said with a quick smile. I gave him a hug and then went to say goodnight to the girls. But later, as I was drifting off to sleep, God brought his words back to my mind, and just wouldn't let them fade.

I thought back over the day, and how Ben had spent most of the afternoon organizing and polishing his rocks and shells. He had displayed them proudly on his bookshelf for all of us to see. I remembered him holding one up and saying, "This one's my favorite. I'm the only one who can touch it because it's so special to me." And then, just hours later, he had said those precious words to me that I was just too busy to comprehend: "Mom, I love you *more* than thunder eggs and sand dollars."

You see, Ben doesn't just *like* those things- he *LOVES* them. He is a passionate collector of anything unique. He treasures each and every rock, shell, feather, coin or birds nest he finds. If you threw one of his treasured rocks out into our gravel driveway, he could find it. He knows exactly what they look like.

The next day, after I dropped the kids off at school, I walked through his room. I looked at every single treasure that was so special to my five-year old. As the Lord spoke to my heart, I was hit by a sudden realization. Ben was telling me a lot more than just I love you. He was also declaring how important I was to him. I was more important to him than his stuff.

All I could think about was, "Can I say the same about God, my Heavenly Father?" Can I honestly say, "I love you God more than my family, my time, my friends, hobbies, TV shows, or even my computer?" Those things are all special in my life, and that's ok. I love my family, I treasure my friends, and I enjoy having hobbies. But do I love God *more* than all of these other things?

I thought about what I put up on a pedestal, what I take the time to polish and put on display. If someone asked my kids "What is important to your mom?", I'm just not sure what their answer would be. And that was very humbling.

I would hope that the answer would come easily to them. I would want them to respond quickly, without even hesitating, "My mom loves God and she loves me with her whole entire heart." That would be amazing, because that's my deepest desire- I want my kids to understand how important God is in my life, and how important they are to me.

The problem is, we have a lot of distractions. We're tired. We have a million things running through our minds at any given moment. We have people we need to take care of, work we have to do, dinners to make, and bills to pay. There are countless excuses not to spend time in prayer. But God wants a deeper relationship with is. He wants us to grow and mature in Him. He wants us to shake things up, and prioritize what's important.

When I turn off the TV and open up my Bible, I am choosing time with God. I am making my relationship with Christ a priority. I am doing just what Ben did to me; I'm throwing my arms around my Savior and saying, "God, I love you more than thunder eggs and sand dollars."

I know He feels the same way about me.

Welcome to My World

The kids and I had planned to go to the park with some friends. We were running behind and it was getting close to lunchtime. So I asked Emma if she would be in charge of packing the lunches. She was *really* excited- like jumping up and down excited. You would have thought I had just given her a million dollars. I mean, what eight-year old girl doesn't like to be in charge, right?

As I headed to take a quick shower, I could already hear her taking orders and banging around in the kitchen. It felt very good to delegate a job to someone else, and I was pretty sure I would be doing it more often.

I jumped in the shower and by the time I was dressed I could here yelling coming from the kitchen. *Lots* of yelling. I crept down the hallway and listened in on pure chaos. Emma was on a stepping stool, trying desperately to put peanut butter on pieces of bread. Katie was hanging on her leg yelling, "Juice, Emma, juice," at the top of her lungs. Ben was on a chair trying to reach his lunchbox from on top of the fridge. He was whining, "Emma, help me get this down" over and over again.

I could tell Emma was trying to tune them out, totally focused on making the sandwiches. Then, all of the sudden, she slammed down the jam jar and yelled at the top of her lungs, "Does it look like I have three hands? I can't do everything at once all by myself! I'm not a superwoman!"

Music to my ears. I stood in the hallway savoring my solitude for a couple more minutes. Then I took a deep breath and walked into the kitchen. I gave her a big hug as the noise continued around us. "Mom, this is so hard," she whimpered, "everybody is loud and bossy and impatient! I can't get anything done!"

I hugged her a little tighter and then whispered into her ear these four words- "Welcome to my world."

Ben: "Mom, I have a new best friend at school!"
Me: "That's awesome! What's his name?"
Ben: "I have no idea."

For the Love of Jesus

Dave and I like to go treasure hunting. Well, let me clarify that a little. *He* likes to go treasure hunting; I go along strictly for the veto power. We sell our finds on eBay, and it's fun because the whole family can get in on the action. We check out Value Village, Goodwill, and the Salvation Army looking for that 'diamond in the rough.'

The kids love to come along, and I don't mind that-most of the time. But after a couple of "embarrassing" moments at garage sales, we knew we needed to come up with a better plan. It's very hard to fly under the radar at a garage sale when your kids are constantly yelling out, "Hey! Will this make a bunch of money on eBay? It's so cheap!" They were ruining our negotiating power and creating a scene- not a good tactic at all.

So, in the parking lot of Value Village one afternoon, we explained to them that we needed a code word. Something they could say to us when they found something cool. We told them to think about it as we walked around, and they could each come up with their own word. They loved the idea.

Into the store we went. It was a busy day with lots of people looking for deals. About five minutes in, I heard a commotion from two aisles over. "Mom, for the love of Jesus!" Ben yelled over the noise. I wasn't sure if I had heard him right-did he just say that? And apparently he didn't think I had heard him either, because he yelled loudly again, "Mom, for the love of *JESUS!*"

As I came around the corner there he stood, smile on his face and beer stein in his hand. "Ben," I whispered, "why are you yelling that?"

He shrugged and said, "It's my code word I chose. Isn't it cool?" Now, I'm not ashamed that he speaks the name of Jesus in public, but it did draw quite a few stares. And the purpose of the code word was *NOT* to do that.

But it had to do with Jesus, and that trumps it all. There was no way I was telling him he couldn't use the name of Jesus as his code word. So, if you're ever in a discount store and hear those words, come on down and join Ben's revival.

.

Diapers Anonymous

When Katie was two and a half, she had absolutely no interest in potty training. She was actually a little scared of the toilet, which made things very complicated. One day I decided to stay home and let her run around in underwear- I was hoping she would eventually give in. After her third accident I sat her down to try and talk to her about it.

"You want to be a big girl right?" I said. She nodded yes. "Well, do you know that some of your best friends already use the toilet? They're big kids now and don't have to wear any diapers!"

She gave me a sideways glare and shrugged her shoulders.

"Your friends Charlie, Anika, Jessica and Payton ALL use the toilet," I continued with excitement in my voice. "Don't you want to be a big kid like them?" I asked.

She stared me down and said with determination, "But Mommy, my name is Katie Hughes. And I don't use the potty."

She would have made a great spokeswoman for DA- also known as Diapers Anonymous.

Katie: "Mom, can you make me a sandwich?"
Me: "Sure, what kind do you want?"
Katie: "Just one that's delicious."

The Flu

I had been sick with the flu for five days. At first, Dave *had* to stay home with me- he had no choice. I couldn't even open my eyelids. I felt like I had been run over by a freight train. I only got up off of the couch to pee, and that took me about half an hour. It was absolutely awful.

But by day three, Dave had to go back to work. And that's when everything got a whole lot worse. If you've ever had the knock-down-drag-out flu *and* had to take care of kids at the same time, I salute you. That, my friends, is a true test in survival. It's bad enough to lay in complete agony, hoping you won't puke up the two Saltine crackers you barely choked down. But then add three loud children to the scenario, and you've got yourselves a bad situation.

I basically crawled from room to room, dragging my blankets behind me. I would collapse in exhaustion and lay perfectly still while they climbed on me and sang 'get better' songs at the top of their lungs. They watched 800 movies and I didn't care. I was just praying I would make it through the day. I'm not sure who fed them- it was probably me, but I don't remember. I'm pretty sure they subsisted on Pop Tarts and string cheese, because those were both gone when I finally came back to my senses.

Finally, on day six, I was going to try to leave the house. I still felt very weak, but I knew the kids and I desperately needed some fresh air and a change of scenery. We were all going completely crazy. I spent the morning lying on the floor trying to conserve energy. I was mentally planning what errands we needed to run and calculating how many hours until Dave would be home.

Around one o'clock, we finally drove away from the house for the first time in six days. I want to clarify that I had absolutely NO INTENTION of getting out of the car. You'll understand why I'm clearing that up right away. My goal was to drive around running errands with the windows down. Everything I needed to do could be done from the car. We had to drop off library books, deposit a check, mail some bills, and stop by the coffee shop drive-thru.

Because I had no intention of actually interacting with people, I didn't spend too much time getting ready. In fact, I don't think I even tried. Have you ever seen someone who's had the flu for five days? There's absolutely no way to make that face look pretty. My whole entire outfit consisted of rubber boots, sweats, a tank top and an old hoodie sweatshirt. No makeup had touched my face in days, maybe a week if I'm honest. My face was pale and I hadn't even taken a shower. Come to think of it, I'm surprised my kids even set foot outside with me.

We crossed everything off of our list, and we all seemed to be in better spirits. We were on our way to the coffee shop when I suddenly remembered that we were out of milk and laundry soap. We needed both of these things really bad. Without thinking, I pulled into the Fred Meyer parking lot. I'm going to blame it on the cold medicine, but I honestly forgot how scary I looked.

I proceeded to walk right into Fred Meyer looking like that. I marched through the aisles with not a care in the world. We got the milk and laundry soap, and then just for fun, I thought I would let the kids pick out a doughnut. It wasn't until Ben sprayed hot chocolate all over the glass doughnut case that I came crashing back to reality.

Maybe it was the stares from other customers that triggered it, or maybe it was the look of pity I got from the bakery manager. Whatever it was, I suddenly remembered how awful I looked. I started to make an escape plan, and even considered ditching the milk and laundry soap and making a run for it.

Then, to make matters even worse, something surfaced from deep within my subconscious. I had a flashback to that morning. I remembered sitting on the floor letting Emma and Katie do my hair. Gasp! My hands reached up to feel my hair, and sure enough-I had never taken it out! My hair was in three different braids, going out in three different directions. I had one scrunchie up high, four barrettes holding in the loose strands, and a big pink bow on top. I felt panic setting in as I looked down at my sweats and rubber boots combo.

I took a deep breath. The bakery manager was still cleaning up Ben's hot chocolate, and somehow I had to make it through the checkout line. I leaned over and whispered to the kids, "We have to get out of here fast- I look *horrible!*" Katie just smiled and touched my face. She said, "But I think you look beautiful mommy!"

I pasted on a smile as I went through the check out line. Most people avoided eye contact anyway; I'm pretty sure they thought I was crazy. We almost made it to the exit when an older lady stopped me. "I just wanted you to know that your hair is lovely," she said a smile.

"See, Mommy?" Katie said happily, "I told you."

My advice? Don't ever leave your house when you have the flu- there's just no good outcome to that at all.

"Ben won't let me love him today. I just want to love him." -Katie Hughes

The Worst Dream of All

At 4am I was nudged (not too gently) awake by the little boy of the house. He stood by the bed with crocodile tears in his eyes and sweat beads on his forehead. "I had a bad dream," he whispered as he climbed onto the bed to snuggle with me.

"What was it about?" I mumbled sleepily.

He said, "There were these HUGE monsters and they came into our house!"

"Wow, that's really scary, what did they do?" I asked.

He grabbed my face with his little hands and said with a quivering voice, "It was so awful, mommy. They came into the house and took *both* our TV's! I had nothing to watch in the morning!" And with that, he buried his face in the pillow and cried himself back to sleep.

Mama Bird

Katie was helping me make cookies. I was measuring ingredients and she was dumping it in the bowl. I was also making dinner at the same time, which I would highly not recommend *ever*. I was a little distracted and frazzled, but we were having fun anyway.

We had just dumped in the flour and turned on the mixer. I turned my back for just a minute to stir the taco meat and that's when I heard it: a thump-thump-thumping sound coming from the Kitchenaid. I turned and saw Katie staring into the bowl with a panicked look on her face. The bowl was doing it's own little crazy dance.

"What did you do?" I asked as I ran over to turn off the mixer.

She looked into the bowl, and then touched my face with her butter-covered hands and said, "Please don't be mad at me, Mama Bird."

I wasn't mad. How could I be mad when she calls me Mama Bird with flour streaks across her face and chocolate chip lips? I investigated the dough and fished out a plastic spoon and measuring cup. They didn't look so good. Another lesson learned- never turn your back on a three-year old.

If You Sat on Me I Would Die

We all know that kids are brutally honest. Not a day goes by that they keep their opinions to themselves. One morning I might look in the mirror and think, "Dang, I am looking pretty hot right now," only to be told five minutes later by my three- year old that I'm "huge compared to her." This is so good for my self- esteem.

Here's a few of my absolute favorite 'opinions' my kids have felt necessary to tell me over the years:

"It still looks like there's a baby in your tummy."

"You smell."

"Your hair looks like gross noodles."

"If you sat on me I would die."

"You should wear prettier shoes."

"Maybe you should go running like that lady."

"This chicken doesn't taste at all like chicken."

"Your breath is so gross."

"You should take a cooking class."

"Do you brush your teeth at all?"

"Are eyebrows supposed to look like that?"

"Did that shirt shrink, or what?"

"Are girl legs usually hairy like that?"

I could go on and on, but I feel my self-esteem plummeting even as I type this. I think you get the idea- and if you've been around kids at all, you've been there too.

Kids just have this overwhelming need to let you know what's on their mind. It's like they have a polygraph machine in their head that forces them to tell the truth no matter what. What do you think of your mom's hair? Oh, it looks a little crazy? You better tell her. See that lady on aisle three at Fred Meyer with the really bad sunburn? You better announce loudly that she should have used more sunscreen. Oh, and that guy waiting in line at Subway? I think it's a great time to tell your mom that he looks like a woman.

All day long this goes on. I'm pretty used to it by now, and it takes a lot to faze me. In all honestly, I left the rest of my pride on the operating table almost four years ago. Dave tells it like this: the nurse was leading him down the hallway towards the room where Katie would soon be born via C-section. As they stopped to put on masks, the doors swung open, and there I was in all my glory. Every single bright light was shining down on me. Not one single piece of clothing on, arms stretched out to my sides and a huge belly sticking straight up- completely naked for everybody to see. It's a good thing he loves me- a *LOT*. That just is not a pretty sight.

When you're having a baby someone's always asking your weight, taking your pee, telling you to undress, feeling your boobs, and asking what foods your eating. By kid number three my pride had long been left at the curb.

But still, sometimes it's nice not to have every little thing pointed out to me all the time. We constantly try to reinforce the idea of a *positive* compliment, but sometimes THAT even backfires. Like when Emma told someone that there teeth were "a beautiful shade of yellow," or when Ben told me, "This dinner isn't as gross as last night."

They try. They really do. And that brings me to a couple months ago, when I decided to take an evening bike ride with the kids. Earlier that day, we had talked (again) about how to choose our words carefully, and focus on the positive in people. I was pretty confident it had sunk in this time. And now we were out enjoying the fresh air and having a wonderful time.

I was in front pulling Katie in the trailer, Emma was right behind me and Ben brought up the rear. About halfway through our ride Emma yelled out, "Hey mom, I can't even see your bicycle seat with your butt on it! It's like magic! How do you do that?" Awesome. I could hardly pedal I was so self-conscious after that. I felt like every person we passed from then on out was staring at my huge gigantic butt hanging off the seat.

I knew she didn't mean to crush my self-esteem into tiny pieces. She was just being a kid. I just thank the good Lord everyday that He's keeping me humble and I pray that I will still have some shred of pride left when they leave for college.

Frozen Food Aisle

I was halfway down the frozen food aisle, trying to decide which Popsicle's to buy. The freezer door was open, Ben was begging for ice cream sandwiches and Katie was making handprints on the fogged up glass.

I have no idea what possessed Ben to do what I was about to witness. Out of the blue he decided to lick the shelf inside the freezer. I have no words. And of course, it got stuck. He froze in what I'm only assuming was instant panic and regret all rolled into one. A few seconds passed where I could only stare at him and think "did he just lick that frozen shelf?"

Before I even had time to think about what to do, he yanked his tongue off, leaving some of his poor skin behind. Some blood followed. Some screams followed. Some stares followed. I tried to paste on my stressed- out mommy smile that I'm sure freaks people out. I searched frantically in my purse for some napkins, and finally came up with an old tissue. It would have to do.

He held the tissue to his tongue and we tried to leave the scene as quickly as possible. Luckily no frustrated words from me were even necessary. I actually never said anything until we got to the car. He had stopped crying and finally said, "I'm not sure why I did that, but I'm never doing it again." Lesson learned.

Seriously?

Katie and I were waiting to check in at the doctor's office. The line was pretty long and she was getting antsy, so I picked her up. She kept herself entertained by fiddling with my necklace and earrings, and pretty soon it was our turn.

"We're here for an appointment at 1:30," I said to the woman behind the counter.

Right at that exact moment, Katie decided that it was the perfect time to announce very loudly, "I really like your big girl boobies mommy!"

I should be used to being embarrassed in every social situation by now. But my face still turned red in nothing flat. The lady tried to hide her smile as I calmly said back, "Thank you Katie, but let's not talk about mommy's boobies right now." Good grief.

Katie: "I wish I was pretty like you."

Ben: "It's called handsome, Katie, not pretty."

Katie: "Oh, I wish I was handsome like you."

Ben: (with frustration) "No, I'm handsome and you're pretty!"

Katie: "I don't feel pretty today."

Ben: "Listen. You don't have to worry, Kate. God made us all handsome or pretty. Even if you were all muddy and naked He would still think you're pretty, ok? That's how it is."

Katie: "Ok, I'm pretty."

Ben: "Now go away because I need some space!"

My Apologies to Convenience Stores Everywhere

I have seen a lot of crazy things these past ten years. I've walked into a room to find my six- month old baby rolling across the carpet leaving a trail of diarrhea in his wake. I've found marker all over the walls and furniture. I've seen my kids eat dog food. I've dropped off my seven-year old daughter at school in her tinker bell snuggie because that's all she wanted to wear. I've seen my fine china teacups thrown across the room and shatter into little pieces. I've found Lego's in the toilet and pinecones under my pillow. I've walked into the kitchen to find my two-year old making snow angels with a box of spilled rice crispy cereal. I've watched our son crawl under a restaurant table to get his shoe and come back up chewing gum- that was *not* his.

But nothing had prepared me for what was about to go down that hot summer evening of 2011. I thought I had seen it all, but I was in for a pretty wild ride. Like usual, the hours leading up to the 'incident' were absolutely wonderful. I was actually feeling pretty on top of my game as a mom. Whenever you get that feeling, just know that very soon you will come crashing hard back to reality.

We had just enjoyed four fun- filled days of vacation and it was time to head back home. We had two cars, so the boys piled in one and I took the girls with me. Everyone was happy; Emma and Katie were laughing in the backseat and taking turns playing the Ipod.

About an hour into the drive, Katie (who was almost two at the time) started to whimper. Then she started to cry. I turned on some soft music and waited for her to fall asleep. That did not help at all. When her crying got worse, I tried giving her some crackers and a sippy cup of water. Nothing was working.

Thirty minutes later Emma announced that she had to go potty, and since we all needed a break from the crying, I pulled off at the next gas station. After I parked, Emma jumped out and I unbuckled Katie from her car seat. She stopped crying and smiled at me- I was suddenly glad that I had made the decision to stop.

We entered the convenience store to find a long line for the bathrooms. "Mom, I have to go right now," Emma whined as she danced around. Just as I started to tell Emma she would have to wait, I felt Katie's entire body go stiff. Her face got really pale and before I could do anything she started to projectile vomit- everywhere. Her head was facing over my shoulder and the rack of chips and pepperoni took a direct hit.

Time seemed to slow down as I watched three people run for the exit. I saw Emma plug her ears and plaster herself against the refrigerator doors. The teenage boy ringing people up was looking at me in horror. When she turned her head and puked on a case of soda, I knew what I had to do. I held her out in front of me and tried to use my body as a human vomit shield. It just kept coming and coming. It was pouring down me and puddling up on the floor.

When the gagging sounds finally stopped, I looked up to see that the line for the bathroom had parted like the Red Sea. A precious old lady was holding the door open for us while holding a handkerchief to her nose. Ten feet sure seems like a long way when you're leaving a trail of puke behind you.

I did my best to clean her up. There was no hope for me, unless I stripped down naked and ran for the car. But I figured I had scarred those poor people enough already. About five minutes later we emerged to find the store mostly emptied out- everyone had run for their lives. There were only three who remained: the poor kid cleaning up the aftermath of Katie's vomit tornado, and two seasoned truck drivers who stood waiting at the counter munching on pork rinds. They've seen it all, you know.

I walked by the store clerk, and offered the most sincere apology I could while covered in throw-up. I was on the verge of tears. He mumbled something I couldn't comprehend, but I think he was just trying not to look directly at me. I didn't blame him at all.

As I made my way to the exit, one of the truckers walked over to me. He patted Emma on the head and said in a gruff voice "Don't worry, honey, we've all got kids and we've all been there". I would have hugged him right then and there if I hadn't smelled like a sewer. He opened the door for me and I walked outside with my head hung low and a tear-streaked face.

The people who had run from the store mid-puke were waiting silently by their cars. I didn't dare look back as we made our way to the car. As I buckled Katie into her car seat, I glanced at Emma. She still had her ears plugged and had lost most of the color in her face.

"Are you ok, Emma?" I yelled to get her attention. She unplugged her ears just long enough to scream, "I knew I should have ridden with dad!" And then she broke down in sobs. I rolled down all the windows, got back on the freeway and drove the rest of the way home covered in vomit. As for Katie, she fell instantly asleep. I guess she felt a lot better.

In the Midst of Tragedy

Every once in awhile, I just need to pull my kids close. I'm not talking about hugs and kisses; we do that every single day. This is something very different. There's something deep inside of us that simply longs to protect our children from the evil of the world. The mother hen in us comes out and we just *need* to gather our chicks and pull them under our wings. In the midst of tragedy, we understand more clearly what is important.

I remember waking up to the phone ringing on September 11th. My mom's voice was shaky on the other end of the line: "Turn on your TV," she said, "Something's happened." The whole world was shocked. It was unbelievable and absolutely heartbreaking.

Even though we lived far away from New York City, and even though I was in college, my mom needed to see me. She longed to pull me into her arms. She needed to hold my sisters and I close, even just for a moment. She was our mom, and in the face of uncertainty, she still wanted to protect us.

Four years later, I got another call from her. I was putting some groceries away and quickly picked up the phone. "Hey!" I said happily. "What are you doing?"

Silence. And then my world came crashing down around me. "We lost your dad," she whispered tearfully. I couldn't comprehend what she was saying.

"What do you mean?" I asked her.

"He passed away," she tried to say through her tears, "I found him...out back by the garden. He's gone." I listened to her cries on the other end of the phone. I felt like I couldn't breathe, like the air had been sucked right out of me.

"No," I yelled into the phone, "NO! I just talked to him a few hours ago. He was laughing! I JUST talked to him." I sunk down onto the floor and started sobbing.

"Nikki," I heard softly from the receiver, "I need you to come home right now." The two-hour drive seemed to take days. When I pulled up to the house, there she stood with my sister, filled with grief, waiting to gather me in her arms. My other sister was in Africa when she got the call, and I can only image how painfully long those flights home were. When the four of us were finally together, we held each other and cried. For a long, long time.

In crisis, we need each other. In devastating circumstances, we need each other. It doesn't make the pain go away, but it brings us comfort in the midst of tragedy. Since I've had kids, I've experienced this longing a few times. Devastating earthquakes, tsunamis and hurricanes have claimed hundreds of thousands of lives. Terrorist attacks, bombings, and airplane crashes fill the news hour. Loved ones have been diagnosed with cancer. People I love have died.

I remember sitting in my son's kindergarten classroom on December 14th. His class was having a Christmas party when we heard the devastating news coming out of Newtown, Connecticut. I gathered him into my arms and didn't let go. The rest of the afternoon I wouldn't let my kids out of my sight, and wept for the parents who would not be hugging their children that day.

I can't stop bad things from happening. I can't shelter my kids from everything that is evil. But I can comfort them when they don't understand. I can hold them in the midst of uncertainty. I can gather them in my arms when their grief is too much to bear.

I think we sometimes forget that God feels the same way about us. We are his children, and He loves us. He wants us to run into his loving arms when we're scared. He is tender- hearted towards us and longs for time with us. He is our refuge in times of trouble. Psalms 91:4 says, "He will cover you with his feathers, and under his wings you will find refuge; his faithfulness will be your shield and rampart."

How amazing is that? God did not promise us a life without hardships. But He is always there to be our refuge. He never lets us out of his sight. He weeps with us. He is there when everything is falling apart. His loving arms are outstretched and waiting. When the world makes absolutely no sense, and tragedy is tearing at our heart and soul, we can run to Him. He knows exactly how we feel, and He will pull us under His wings in the midst of the storm.

"I've been talking so much today that I can't even hear myself think anymore."- Emma Hughes

Hyperlink

"Girls, come down here right now, " my mom yelled from the bottom of the staircase, "we need a family meeting!" We froze. It didn't sound like a very fun meeting. We were all busy getting reports written, math homework done, and talking on the phone. All of the important things teenagers do.

We looked at each other and shrugged as we trudged down the stairs. We were suspicious. We didn't know what this family meeting was about. It was one of those sneak attack meetings that come with absolutely no warning. I was racking my brain and couldn't come up with anything I had done lately to warrant this kind of formality.

We reached the bottom of the staircase and there stood my mom, holding a piece of paper in her clenched hand. And there at the table sat my dad, no hint of a smile anywhere on his face. It was not looking good for us. I decided to break the silence. "So, what's going on?" I asked nonchalantly. Probably not the best angle in retrospect.

"I'm not sure what's going on", my mom said holding up the piece of paper, "But we intend to find out!"

I quickly exchanged glances with my sisters. And then panic started to set in. I could see that they looked worried too. We might be willing to take a bullet for each other out in the real world, but at home we were easily capable of throwing each other under the bus.

"First of all," my mom said, "I want to know who can tell me what a hyperlink is?"

Uncomfortable silence followed. I was a senior in high school at this point, and probably should have known what a hyperlink was. But I didn't. I made a mental note that I needed to pay better attention in computer class.

Crystal looked even more clueless than I felt. Alicia looked a little confused, but then proudly announced; "I know what a hyperlink is. We learned about them at school."

My parents just stared at her, with a mixture of shock and dismay. Inwardly I breathed a huge sigh of relief; Alicia had successfully thrown *herself* under the bus this time.

"What's the big deal?" Alicia asked again, still not quite sure what the problem was.

"The big deal," my mom replied, "Is that someone has been looking at a porn site on our computer through a hyperlink!"

I think if we had possessed any kind of superhuman powers, we would have used them to transport ourselves out of that kitchen. Right out of the conversation to a happier place- a place where the word porn was never spoken out loud by our parents. But there we stood, with no place to run.

Alicia stood in stunned silence. Like a deer caught in the headlights. Man, I felt sorry for her. Sort of. I also found the whole thing really funny and apparently couldn't wipe the stupid smile off my face.

"Do you think this is funny?" My dad asked looking directly at me. I always tend to incriminate myself for no good reason.

I thought about saying, "No, I don't think it's funny at all," but as God is my witness I couldn't stop the laughter from coming. "It's kinda funny," I said with a smile.

"What's funny about it?" He said back.

"It just is," I said trying to hold it together. Crystal was on the verge of giggling too, but Alicia looked pretty devastated.

"So, who here looked at porn?" My mom asked again.

"I didn't look at porn!" Alicia insisted, the tears flowing freely.

"Me either!" Crystal said.

I shook my head and said, "It wasn't me either."

"Well, somebody was looking at porn, because it was reported to us!" My mom said with frustration.

"We're serious! It wasn't us." We looked at each other and knew it was true.

My mom knew it too. And so did my dad. But the evidence was right there in her hand, so none of it made sense. They sent us back upstairs. We walked away, somewhat stunned that we had just been in a room with our parents where the word porn was spoken out loud. It just felt...weird.

The next day the mystery was solved. After talking to many customer service agents, it was determined that our computer had been hacked. The pornography had been accessed through our computer from a remote location. We were in the clear.

In the end we all came out mostly unscathed. Alicia's reputation was not tarnished after all. We still remained somewhat innocent. I had learned what a hyperlink was. My parents could take a big sigh of relief.

The only bad news? My mom could no longer call a family meeting without someone saying, "Is it about porn again?"

Meatball Madness

Katie was sitting at the table coloring while I was making spaghetti sauce. "What are you doing, mom," she asked me.

"I'm making spaghetti and meatballs for dinner tonight," I said.

"Can I have sketti now?" she asked.

"Nope, it's for *dinner*," I explained, "you have to take a nap still and then it will be dinner time.

"I don't want to take a nap, I want to eat meatballs!" She yelled jumping up and down. I lifted her up and showed her that they weren't ready yet. That seemed to settle her down.

I tucked her in for her nap and then started to do some laundry. She was quiet for awhile, but then I heard her door open. "I'm ready for those meatballs now mommy!" She screamed in excitement.

"Go get back in bed," I said with frustration, "they're not ready yet!"

About ten minutes later I stood outside her bedroom door. I thought maybe she had fallen asleep, and I started to tiptoe away from her door. That's when I heard something.

I leaned in closer, and heard her whispering over and over again, "I need those meatballs, I need those meatballs so bad!"

The Tree of God

I was on the phone when Ben came running into the room. "Mom, I need a hammer, toilet paper, glue, highlighters, and maybe a couple screws- oh, and marshmallows!"

I was already stressed from listening to the prompts on the other end of the line and speaking one-word answers to *no one*. So I held up my hand and whisper-yelled, "Fine, whatever you need. Can't you see I'm on the phone?"

"Thanks Mom!" He yelled as he ran out of the room. I spent the next few minutes finishing up my phone call with a computer. I hung up, took a deep breath and then it hit me like a freight train. What did he ask me for? A hammer? Toilet paper?

Emma was sitting on the couch reading a magazine. "Did I just tell Ben it was ok to use a hammer and screws?" I asked her.

"Yep, you did," she answered without looking up from her reading. "But you do that a lot. I call it your zone-out moments."

"What's he doing with all that stuff?" I asked her.

"I have no idea," she answered, "but Katie's with him."

I ran outside to find this: Ben standing on a ladder hammering a sign made of toilet paper into a tree. Katie was steadying the ladder with one hand while stuffing marshmallows into her mouth with the other. Little bits of glue and bark dust covered her dress. Their explanation? It was the tree of God and needed to be labeled as such. And to do this project, they needed to eat lots of marshmallows for energy.

After this incident, I made a new rule that no one could ask me an important question while I was on the phone. That lasted all of four hours.

Ben: "I want to be a missionary when I grow up!"

Me: "That's awesome! What do you think you need to do to be a missionary?"

Ben: "I probably need to learn a different language, like maybe English."

The Cool Car

We were using my mom's car for a few days and the kids were pretty excited about it. In fact, when I had announced that we would be trading Nana cars, you would have thought I gave them a trip to Disney World. I guess we just don't have many other exciting things going on.

The second day we had the 'cool car', I had a bunch of errands to run. I told the kids we were leaving and they needed to head outside.

"What?" Emma asked in a panicked voice. "You mean we're leaving right now?"

"Yep," I said as I opened the garage door.

"Then I have to go change!" She said as she ran from the room.

"You look fine," I yelled down the hallway, "let's just go!"

"I'll just be a minute," she yelled back.

I loaded the car with some Goodwill boxes and library books that were due. I buckled Katie into her car seat. Then we sat. And waited. For what seemed like *forever*. Finally, here she came. She had on jeggings, a long sparkly shirt, black high heels, a puffy scarf, glittery hat, and about four bracelets. Her pink sequined purse was hanging from her wrist.

I smiled and said, "What was wrong with your jeans and sweatshirt? You know we're just going to the library, right?"

"Mom," she said as she buckled herself in, "it might be ok to wear comfy clothes in the suburban, but in Nana's car we need to look fancy." She opened up her flip mirror and put on some lip-gloss. "Ok," she said, "I'm ready now."

I stared at her in the rearview mirror. I suddenly felt self-conscious about my lack of make-up and ketchup stained shirt. Hopefully she could handle hanging out with commoners for the afternoon.

"I just love the smell of three-day old band aids." – Emma Hughes

Daydreaming

After one of Ben's baseball games, I asked him if he had a good time.

"Yeah, except the coaches kept asking me over and over and *over* again if I knew where the play was at," he said.

"Well, maybe that's because you weren't paying attention," I said.

"It's because I was daydreaming the whole time," he told me while he crunched on a mouthful of Cheez-its, "that's probably why."

Exactly.

Peaches the Chicken

Last spring, one of our chickens met an untimely death. It was somewhat traumatic for all involved, but especially for a certain six-year old boy. Now, my kids are not naïve to death. Unfortunately, we've faced it head-on a number of times, whether it was people we loved or numerous animals that had become our friends. And they do realize (to some degree) that every time they eat a beloved chicken nugget or grilled chicken off the BBQ that those are, in fact, dead chickens.

But, when they become your friends, even a chicken's passing is very hard to take. It didn't die right away, and the kids did everything they could to help the poor thing. Ben quickly created a prayer vigil sign-up sheet so we could all take shifts to pray for Peaches. Emma used color-coded markers to create a graph with sign-ups for bringing food and water. They took turns sitting with Peaches until it was time for bed.

Dave and I knew the chicken wouldn't make it. But we did sign up for a shift on the prayer vigil- it was the right thing to do. The next morning, we explained that Peaches did not make it through the night. Emma and Katie seemed somewhat reflective, but then asked for Toaster Strudels and cartoons- they seemed to be ok with the whole thing.

But Ben immediately went and got another sheet of paper and began drawing pictures. "Are you ok, buddy?" We asked him, "What are you doing?"

"I'm planning Peaches funeral. We'll have to have it tonight before my baseball practice," he said very seriously. "Will you be home in time to help me with the funeral, dad?" He looked up at Dave with his big brown eyes and pen poised. Obviously he was ready to write Dave's duties for said funeral. Dave stared at him for a few seconds of uncomfortable silence- I'm assuming he was trying to choose his words carefully and remember what it felt like to be six.

"I will be home in time," Dave said seriously.

Everyone left for work and school and I forgot about the dead chicken. Until Ben got home and the planning commenced. By 5pm that night, he had everything ready- a table set up with flowers, some snacks and ice water, and a little wooden cross. He sat soberly in his black baseball pants and black shirt, just waiting for Dave to get home.

Every once in awhile, he would poke his head into the house and say, "Tell the girls it needs to be quiet in here before the funeral." He meant business.

I was trying to occupy myself with making dinner, but it's hard to feel very sad about the chicken when you're making chicken enchiladas for dinner. I probably should have thought that one out a little better. Finally Dave got home and we all filed out into the backyard.

A hole had already been dug and Peaches lay wrapped in an old towel with just her head sticking out.

Dave said, "Ben, why don't you lay Peaches in the hole now."

"Wait, dad," he said quickly, "I need one more picture with her to remember her by." He gently picked her up. Dave and I exchanged confused glances and I just shrugged my shoulders, mostly just wanting to get this over with.

Dave pulled out his phone and said, "Ok, one picture." I expected a picture with a somewhat somber tone, but Ben smiled his biggest smile while holding that dead chicken up in the air. I sincerely hoped that he wasn't going to ask me to frame it for him.

Then, as he went to lay the chicken in the hole, he flipped it over and her other eye was wide open. "She's ALIVE!" screamed Katie at the top of her lungs. Emma started jumping up and down yelling, "She's not dead, Ben! She's not dead!" All chaos broke loose as Ben quickly set her on the ground to investigate.

"Dad, her eye is open!" He screamed. "I think she made it!" Darn freaky chicken eye. Dave quickly de-escalated the situation by explaining, once again, that the chicken was indeed dead.

We buried her and then stood in awkward silence. I could tell the girls were bored with the whole situation, and we needed to move on. I was ready to walk back inside when Ben said: "Now we can each say a memory or a little prayer."

I could feel the giggles welling up inside me, but there was no way I was letting them out. Emma and Kate both said a little prayer, and I'm pretty sure Katie's included, "Thank you God for this food" but I'm not entirely sure. I was just trying not to lose it. When Dave's turn came, he said seriously, "I'll pass on this one."

Ben took a big deep breath and said, "Ok, I guess I'll pray then." He bowed his head down and this is what he said: "Thank you God for Peaches, she was a very fun chicken to play with. We will miss her and we are all heartbroken."

I couldn't stop it from coming. A giggle escaped my lips and I quickly put my hands to my face to muffle it. Ben looked up fast and I dipped my head down. He came over and grabbed my hand, "Now mom's crying," he said to Dave. Dave took off for the house and barely got the slider door closed before he started laughing. "Where's dad going?" He asked seriously.

"I think Dad just needs some time alone," I managed to say through my hands that were still covering my face.

Ben seemed satisfied that we were all feeling so much emotion. "The funeral is over now," he said, "thank you for coming."

In the weeks following this dramatic event, life slowly went back to normal. And just so you know- we did get a new chicken to take Peaches place, and her name is Little Chocolate Campfire. Don't ask - I have no idea why that's her name.

"I'm so sorry you're not as good at driving as daddy is."-Katie Hughes

What are you Doing in There?

I had only been in the bathroom for thirty seconds when I heard a knock on the door. "Mom, are you in there?" Katie asked. They had been watching a cartoon, but apparently the sound of the bathroom door closing alerted them that they might need something. And they found me- that fast.

I didn't answer because I was mad. Mad that they couldn't just leave me alone long enough so I could go to the bathroom by *myself*. Mad that I no longer had any personal space. I was just plain mad.

"Mom!" They said loudly, "what are you doing?"

"What do you think I'm doing?" I asked with frustration.

"I don't know, but we need some juice," Ben said.

I finally said in a freaky kind of growling voice, "I am going to the bathroom, leave me ALONE!" Silence- for all of ten seconds. Then I heard whispering and lots of giggling. They shoved a comb under the bathroom door- then a quarter. And a matchbox car. A pretty purple bracelet was shoved under next as a little voice yelled, "For you mom!" Roars of laughter followed as they ran away from the door. I was trying to decide whether to laugh or cry when I suddenly had a flashback.

I was transported back to 1987. Three little girls stood outside of a bathroom door, trying to open it with the top of a pen cap. My mom was on the other side of the door, just trying to go to the bathroom in peace. She was mad, frustrated, and very tired.

"Girls, go play," I remember her saying. We were giggling and totally clueless as to why she would be so mad. After going through four different size pen caps, we finally got the right fit. I swung the door open and we all yelled, "Ta-da!" in perfect unison. We were so proud of ourselves. She just hung her head in defeat.

I waited in the bathroom until I was sure they had gone back to their cartoon. Then I tiptoed out and called my mom. "Mom, I'm so sorry," I said. "I'm sorry for the 1980's, and how we never let you go to the bathroom in peace. I understand now. And it's just not cool at all."

She remembered that day. And many others like it. "It's a good thing I loved you girls a lot," she said. "You were worth it."

"Well, if it makes you feel any better," I said, "your grandkids are paying me back big-time."

Busted

While Katie was climbing up into her car seat one afternoon, I tried to sneak a few of her whoppers out of the box- I didn't think she saw me. I tried to chew quietly as I buckled her up; I didn't want to incriminate myself. She was staring intently at me and I was avoiding eye contact at all cost. She finally said in a very serious tone, "Mommy, you are now on my naughty list for sneaking my whoppers." She was shaking her head in disbelief and clutching her box of candy for dear life.

I was busted- by a three- year old.

Band-Aid Wrappers

I was putting Band-Aids on a couple of Katie's toes. As I opened one up, she would take the trash and line it up on the counter. After all was said and done, there was a pretty long line of Band-Aid wrappers. "Mommy," she said, "can I keep all of these wrappers, please?"

I wasn't sure what to say. "What are you going to do with them?" I asked her.

"I'm going to have a collection of them in my room," she stated like it was the most normal thing in the world.

Since I felt bad that she wasn't feeling good I said, "Sure, go for it."

She clapped her hands with excitement and yelled happily, "Thank you mom for making all my dreams come true!" Then she hugged me and ran off.

I am going to save a lot of money on Christmas presents for her.

Camping

Camping with kids is not a vacation. Sure, it's a change of scenery, but it's absolutely not relaxing at all. Do you make awesome memories? Of course. Do I want my kids to experience the great outdoors in all its amazing glory? Yes, I do. Do I love my husband and his intense desire to live off the land and build fires? Absolutely. But do I love camping? Absolutely not.

To me, the words camping and vacation should never go together in the same sentence. A vacation, in my opinion, is supposed to make your life *easier*. Camping is more about the *experience*. When you choose to go camping for a vacation, it's like saying, "Hey, we're going to go to this amazing place and not sleep at all! We're going to have to spend more time cooking than we do at home! You're going to wash dishes with freezing cold water that comes out of a tiny little spicket! You get to use these cool pit toilets and dodge spiders while you pee! You don't even have to take the time to shower, isn't that amazing? And best of all, when your baby wakes up in the middle of the night, you get to warm up milk over a fire instead of using a microwave! It's going to be wonderful!"

Don't get me wrong, not all of it is negative. Some of our very best family memories have happened while camping. We've hiked some beautiful mountain trails, seen falling stars, had deep discussions around the campfire, and chased off raccoons at three in the morning. But that doesn't make it a vacation. That makes it an experience we will never forget.

Let's just be real here- it's not fun to go to sleep cold. It's not fun to make four separate trips to the dark, smelly bathrooms during the course of one night. It's not very relaxing to have a two-year old near a fire. It's not fun when a thunderstorm rolls through and you have nowhere to go. It's exhausting trying to find what you need in a gazillion different totes. And it's hard to feel pretty when you're covered in marshmallow, dirt and hot dog grease.

But will I do it again? Yes. I go camping because I love my family and I want to have these wonderful memories. But I don't have to like everything about it. And I don't have to call it a vacation, because it's not. It's an *experience* in survival.

"Ben is making me so mad- I just want to punch him in the face! But since I can't, I'm going to go imagine it in my head!" – Emma Hughes

Out of My Control

On a bitter cold night in early January, Dave and I drove to the hospital. Our little boy was overdue, and the doctors had finally decided to induce. The week before had been very painful- every time I walked, the pain in my pelvis was so strong that I would just about pass out. There was no longer any comfortable way to sleep, and my face was puffy and swollen.

We got situated in the room, and the nurses got me all hooked up to start the induction. Once the Pitocin kicked in, things started happening fast. My water broke and the contractions came on quickly. I got an epidural and for about an hour I was able to relax. I could tell the contractions were happening very frequently; there was so much tightening and pressure.

When I got to about eight centimeters, they started getting the room ready. My mid-wife came in and said, "I'm going to check you and see how things are progressing." All of the sudden the pain was almost unbearable. My epidural was wearing off, and I felt like I was going to pass out. Dave and my mom were both on either side of me, and I remember yelling, "It hurts so bad, I don't think I can do this!"

The mid-wife quickly checked me and told me to push. I tried to focus my energy on bearing down and breathing. But nothing was happening. The pain was so excruciating, and every time I started to push they would tell me to stop. "Turn her over on her side," I heard the mid-wife say. I felt myself being pushed over. "Now, push," she said- nothing. They tried to roll me to the other side. Nothing seemed to be working, and tensions were rising.

That's when I heard one of the nurses say, "We need to call a doctor in here right now."

"I'm going to try one more thing," she replied.

"I'm calling the doctor," the nurse said as she picked up the phone.

The pain was so blinding that I couldn't focus on much. But what I do remember and will never forget was the look on the doctor's face when he entered the room. He looked at me, then at the monitor, and asked, "How long has the baby's heart rate been that low?"

Dave gripped my hand tight as he stared into my eyes. I saw confusion and fear all mixed into one. "I need the forceps right now," the doctor said calmly. I squeezed my eyes shut. I felt like I couldn't hang on much longer.

"This isn't working, and the baby's heart rate is dropping too fast. Prep for an emergency C-section," he barked to everyone in the room. Chaos broke out as I was unhooked from monitors and prepped for surgery. "What's happening?" I asked Dave as panic started to set in.

"I don't know," he replied with a shaky voice. Then they pulled him aside to get dressed for the operating room.

Just before they wheeled me away, my mom grabbed my hand. "I love you darling," she said with tears in her eyes. And then she slipped my dad's ring on my finger and said, "I'll see you soon, ok?"

I drifted in and out of consciousness after that. I remember them lifting me to the operating table. I remember feeling intense pressure as I heard the doctor say, "Making the first incision now."

It was all happening so fast; I couldn't wrap my head around it. My body wanted desperately to fall asleep, but I needed to know if my baby was ok. "God, please, help him be ok," I prayed. Minutes ticked by. And then I heard it- a tiny little cry that was the best sound in the whole world.

They let me look at him, but then he was whisked away. Dave went with him and I was alone. After that, I don't remember much at all. I had no energy left. I finally gave in to the exhaustion and fell into a deep sleep. Dave said that when he came into the recovery room, I was so pale I hardly even looked like myself. It scared him pretty bad.

Finally, the next day, I got to hold Benjamin for the first time. I couldn't sit up, but they laid him next to me. I let my tears flow, thanking God that he was ok. He was perfect, an absolutely beautiful baby. He was also over ten pounds; he had completely gotten himself stuck on his way out.

Four days later we finally got to go home. As Dave and I pulled away from the hospital, we both knew how lucky we were. Things could have gone so different. God's plan is not always our plan. Life can change in an instant. I learned that there are so many things out of my control. Life is precious, and we shouldn't take even one day for granted.

Problem Solver

I got Ben out of the bath one night and then realized we were out of towels. "Wait right here," I told him, "I'm gonna go grab a towel from the dryer."

When I came back thirty seconds later, I saw a very wet and naked boy wrapping himself up with toilet paper. "I solved the problem myself, mom!" He said with a smile.

"Mom, can you hold out this frying pan so I can run full speed into it? I want to see if it leaves a face print." -Ben Hughes

Bilingual

Emma came home one day and announced, " Did you guys know that I speak Spanish and Russian?"

"I did not know that," I said. "Who taught you?"

"I just learn it from listening to my friends at school," she replied.

"Do you talk to them in Spanish and Russian?" I asked nervously.

"Sometimes, but they never understand what I'm saying," she said. "So, mostly I just talk to myself in Spanish now."

What's My Name Again?

We were running late for school one morning and I told the kids they would probably have to sign in at the office. As I pulled up to the front doors for drop-off I turned to Ben (who had never been late before), and said, "Just go stand in line at the office window and then tell them your name and…."

He cut me off mid-sentence. "I know what to do mom," he said confidently as he waved goodbye and followed Emma into the school.

The day flew by and I forgot about the late drop-off. As I tucked him into bed that night he said, "Mom, we really need to practice saying my name."

"What do you mean?" I asked him.

"This morning at the office, they asked me what my name was and I couldn't remember. It was *so* embarrassing!" He stared at me. I was at a loss for words.

"So, what did you say when they asked you?"

"I just said what came into my head- I'm Ben Nicole David. They looked at me kinda funny," he said.

"Sorry buddy, that's rough," I told him.

"That's why we HAVE to practice my name more often!" He said seriously.

"Ok, but I'm pretty sure we've been calling you Ben Hughes for the last six years," I said. "Was that not enough practice?"

"I guess not. It's awful not knowing who you are, mom!"

Paused

I came into the kitchen to see why it was so quiet. Emma was sitting with her arm outstretched over the table, not moving.

I said, "Emma, what are you doing?"
With only her lips moving, she said, "I paused myself."

I'll put Myself on Time Out

I sat down at the computer to just relax for a few minutes. The crazy part of my afternoon was over- kids were picked up from school, snacks had been given, homework folders gone through, and lunch boxes emptied out.

I had been brought up to date on who said what at recess, who got in trouble at circle time, and how interesting learning about fractions is. The neighbor girls had rung the doorbell so I sent everyone outside to play. I knew two loads of laundry needed to be folded, but I also knew I should take advantage of the quiet. I sipped on my iced tea and got caught up on some news.

That's when I heard it. I literally had only been sitting for 3.5 minutes when I heard a loud BANG. I glanced outside and all the kids seemed to be fine-laughing, playing, running around. I went and checked rooms; nothing was out of place. I went and sat back down.

Then, out of the corner of my eye I saw Ben pass by the front window on his way to the garage. He looked…nervous. I heard the garage door open and reluctant footsteps shuffling my way. As he came into the room, his head hung low and his shoulders were drooping. He walked right up to me and stopped. "What's the matter?" I asked.

"Well," he mumbled, "I am definitely going on time-out for this one."

"What did you do?" I asked, almost afraid of the answer.

"I just got way too hyper and I broke the window with a rock. I'm so sorry," he said.

A few seconds of silence passed as I tried to process this news. "I guess you need to go show me," I said as I stood up.

"Okay, I'll show you. But maybe we should hug first," he said as he wrapped his arms around me. Now I was scared.

We walked out front to the other side of the house and there it was- a very broken window, and a little rock laying underneath as evidence. Now my head drooped. I took some very deep breaths. I was about ready to lose my temper when an image suddenly popped into my head:

I'm fifteen years old and I'm pretty into my own awesome self. I had been driving with a permit for almost a year and of course, I thought I was amazing at it. My mom was sitting in the front seat, the music was on and I was feeling well, let's face it- a little too hyper. I took the corner pretty tight as we pulled onto the main road and my mom yelled out, "Nikki, you just hit the mailbox!"

"I did not!" I said back, "I didn't even feel anything!"

"Yes, you did," she said back. "It scraped the side of the car!"

"Did I hit the mailbox?" I glanced back at my two little sisters sitting in the back seat looking like deer caught in the headlights. Being very wise beyond their years, they both sided with my mom.

"Keep going because we don't want to be late- we'll check the car when we get there," my mom said.

"Nothing's going to be there," I replied grumpily. I was absolutely positive I didn't hit that mailbox. The rest of the car ride was eerily quiet.

When we pulled into the parking lot everyone got out. And there, scraped all down the side of the car was the evidence. And my mom's head drooped. And I felt nauseous as I looked at her and saw the frustration in her face. But she didn't yell. She didn't lose her temper. She was disappointed and that was enough for me.

She walked over to me, gave me a hug and said, "Nikki, you have got to be more careful!" We talked about not being too cocky and not letting your excitement overrule common sense. I know I suffered consequences for scraping up the car that day, but I remember feeling loved even though I had done something wrong.

As I stood there staring at the broken window that afternoon, I felt my anger drain away. The little boy standing next to me with tears running down his cheeks was way more important than any old window. He needed to learn from his mistakes, just like I did. "I'll help daddy fix it," he cried, "I promise." I knelt down to give him a hug, and felt like I was going back in time twenty years as I said to him, "I know you will. You have to be more careful, ok?"

We sat and talked about why it happened, and what he did wrong. Then he said, "I'll just go put myself on time-out now."

While walking through Sears one night, we passed a beautiful patio set complete with an umbrella and a string of lights. Katie squealed with delight and said, "Oh, mommy, this is where I'm going to have my next birthday party! Please? Can I?"

Do you think Sears would mind if we rented out their patio set next to the escalators? It would make Katie really happy.

Downloading

Emma came running into the room and stopped right in front of me. "Do you need something?" I asked her.

"Oh, man" she groaned, "I totally just forgot what I was going to say! It was important!"

"I hate it when that happens," I said. "Don't worry, you'll remember in a little while."

She left. A few minutes later I walked by her room with a load of laundry. "Did you remember it yet?" I asked.

"No," she said with frustration, "it's somewhere in my brain but I'm having trouble downloading it right now!"

Head Honcho

We went to the store to get a few needed groceries, and Ben decided to take what was left of his birthday money with him. He had exactly $4.oo hot in his pocket. As I was scanning the magazine racks, I heard an excited squeal of delight.

"Mom, I found The Green Lantern! They have it here!" He came running over clutching the movie to his chest.

"Oh, very cool. But how much is it?" I asked.

"Well, it's ten dollars. But if you buy it for me I *promise with all my heart* to pay you back the extra money." He said this with 100% sincerity in his voice.

I stood leafing through my magazine, avoiding eye contact while contemplating this major decision. "I'm not sure," I finally said, "I'm going to have to talk to the head honcho about this one."

A few quiet seconds passed. Ben was looking up at me wide-eyed. "You mean God?" he whispered. "I sure hope He says yes." He walked to the next aisle over. "You can pray about it now, mom!" He said loudly.

I was talking about Dave. But I was pretty happy that Ben thinks of God as the head honcho, so I didn't say anything.

After all, we can talk to God about anything, right? Even the Green Lantern.

Talking is Boring

We let Emma download a free app on her iPod that allows her to text certain numbers. Basically she can text family and that's about it. She was excited anyway, and couldn't wait to use it. That night she came and plopped down on the couch next to me.

"Hey, mom," she said, "do you want to text back and forth?"

"You mean instead of sitting here and *talking* to each other?"

"Talking is so boring," she explained, "this will be way more fun!"

We texted back and forth most of the night. I finally confiscated the iPod at 9:35pm when she texted to ask if I could bring her some ice water. We all have our limits.

Grossed Out

I was walking down the hallway one night when something caught my eye. Someone had put a bunch of scotch tape on the wall- right at kid level. I knelt down to investigate. I looked very closely at the clear tape and then recoiled in horror. Smears of snot and boogers had been covered over with tape. I quickly stood up before my gagging reflux kicked in.

Who would do such a thing? My children, that's who. They were already asleep so the interrogation would have to wait. As I lay in bed a few minutes later, I tried to rationalize it in my head. Maybe they wiped their snot off on the wall and then panicked? They didn't want to get in trouble so they covered it up with tape? But why not just wipe it off with a towel? And why would they think that CLEAR tape would hide anything? And better yet, why was the snot on the wall in the first place?

As I fell asleep one last thought crept into my head and sent chills down my spine: where else is snot smeared in this house?

Katie: (Standing right by my feet as I was making her dinner): "Are you thinking what I'm thinking mom?"

Me: "I don't know, what are you thinking?"

Katie: "I'm thinking that I want candy corns for dinner."

Me: "No, I wasn't thinking that at all. Sorry."

Katie: "Then I don't want dinner."

"I Believe in You, Mommy"

Katie has struggled with Eczema since she was six months old. She's almost four years old now and it is still a daily battle in our house. There are good days and bad. Even on the good days we have to lather her up with ointment to help relieve the itching. She's a trooper, though. And even when she's covered in band aids and has to wear long pants on a summer day, she's still smiling.

But every once in awhile, a bad day wins out. An eczema flare-up can ruin your day in nothing flat. Our happy little girl gets so uncomfortable in her skin that her smile fades away. This makes me very, very sad.

When she was two years old she had a horrible flare-up. It was summer and even though we had tried to keep her covered in ointment as much as possible, it was hard when everyone else was playing in sprinklers. The eczema covered her legs and feet, and she had also developed a severe diaper rash. Despite our best efforts and several prescriptions, she was waking up every night with blood on her sheets from scratching at her legs.

It was a painful experience to change her diaper, because it hurt her so bad to wipe off the old creams and put on new ones. Her little body would shake so hard and she would scream out in pain. As I changed her, my tears would flow and I would pray for God to give her some kind of relief.

One day it got to be too much. I was tired. I was tired of seeing her in so much pain. I was tired of nothing working. I was so very tired of not being able to help her feel better. As I rubbed the ointment on her skin, she began to whimper. Then she screamed out, "Mommy, stop! You're hurting me! You're *hurting* me!" I started to cry and couldn't stop. I pleaded desperately, "Katie, I'm not doing this to hurt you, I'm trying to make you better. I don't like to see you in so much pain. Do you believe me baby girl?"

She was sobbing and her little body was shaking. She looked into my eyes and whispered, "I believe in you mommy, I believe in you mommy, I believe in you mommy." When I finished putting her new bandages in place, I pulled her into my arms. We sat together on the floor and cried it all out. We cried until we had no tears left. After a few minutes I could feel her body start to relax, the sting was finally wearing off.

As I held her there on the bedroom floor, I was hit by a sudden realization. Life is not easy. It's really hard. And sometimes we feel like our heart is being ripped right out. We feel like everything is falling apart. People we love are taken from us, marriages end in divorce, a friend is diagnosed with cancer, a tsunami kills thousands, we lose our job, and sometimes friends betray us. Sometimes we just don't understand why we're in so much pain.

But there is someone who does. God is right there with us on the floor when no one else is. He's there to carry us when we just don't have the strength to go on. There are times that our heart is hurting so much, and we just want to scream out to God, "Why are you doing this to me? You're hurting me!"

We have a God who loves us- a God who listens to our every cry. He's right there with us, and he's saying, "I'm not doing this to hurt you; you might not understand right now, but I have a plan to make you better and stronger. I don't like to see you in so much pain. Do you believe me?"

During these dark times, when nothing seems to make sense, we can just take one small step of faith. We can whisper through our pain, "I believe in You, I believe in You." My prayer is that we can all cry out to Him, even when we don't understand why the pain is happening. He's listening, even when we're mad and confused. And just like Katie, we can run into his arms, fully knowing that he loves us no matter what shape we are in.

"Hey mom, I hope we're never so poor that we don't even have important things like mustard." -Ben Hughes

Big Rainbow

I was getting ready for church one morning when Emma was two years old. She was playing at the end of the hallway with some blocks while I picked out what to wear. I finally decided on the new sweater I had just bought. It was a little out of my comfort zone; it had different pastel stripes all over it.

I finished getting dressed and then headed down the hall to make breakfast. She looked up at me and her eyes got really big. "Look out," she said, "big rainbow coming."

I promptly turned around and changed. Two-year olds don't lie about stuff like that. They give it to you straight.

Runaway Car

It was a warm fall evening and my family was sitting around the kitchen table catching up on life. I was in college and my sisters were busy with high school, so the days were few and far between that we were all together. The laughter was flowing, and so were the stories.

My dad was telling us about a recent golf game. He suddenly stopped mid-sentence and quickly sucked in his breath.

"What's wrong?" My mom asked as she followed his gaze out the front window.

We all turned to look and each gasped in surprise. Slowly rolling backward down our driveway was my sisters Volkswagen Bug. And it was picking up speed.

"What in the world!" My dad yelled as he jumped out of his chair. He bolted out the front door and down the steps. We were following close behind, but we were all too late. We made it to the driveway just in time to see the VW crash into our big Fir tree. The crash was followed by silence. Painful silence. The five of us stood there in shock. And then slowly, we all turned to look at my sister Crystal. It was, of course, her car.

"Did you forget to put the parking break on?" My dad said slowly, choosing his words carefully and trying to remain calm.

"I didn't even drive it," Crystal protested, "Mom drove it last!"

We turned to look at my mom. Her eyes were as wide as saucers. "Huh, I guess I didn't put the brake on," she said with a look of dismay. "Sure glad the tree was there to stop it!"

He looked at her, and was at a complete loss for words. My sisters and I were trying not to laugh. I mean, it's not every day you see a car rolling away on it's own. But we kept our mouths shut and slowly walked toward the car. Not a word was spoken as we carefully pushed the car away from the tree.

Then my mom looked over at my dad. "You can sure move fast when you need to," she said with the tiniest hint of a smile. "I'm pretty impressed."

He didn't reply. But I did see a little twinkle in his eye. And then we laughed until our stomachs hurt. She could always make him smile, no matter what.

Please, Just Be Quiet

Every once in awhile my brain just shuts down. I'm almost 99.9% sure this is due to the children that live in my house. More often than not, I find myself standing in the middle of a room and can't remember what I'm doing in there. Was I on my way to take a shower? Am I looking for something? Did I have to go to the bathroom? I'm just not sure.

From the moment I wake up till the time I crawl into bed, three precious human beings are talking to me-*constantly*. And usually all at the same time. It's wonderful and amazing and exhausting. Questions are thrown at me left and right. Songs are sung to me at noise levels unfit for human ears. Knock- knock jokes fill the whole left side of my brain and there's just no room left.

I actually had to pull over to the side of the road one day because I thought my head was going to explode. Kate was singing the alphabet over and over and *OVER*. Ben was practicing his whistling and Emma was telling me for the fifth time how she wanted to be an actress. I stopped the car and rested my head on the steering wheel.

It took them almost two minutes to realize we were at a standstill. "What are you doing, mom?" Emma asked.

"I just need a little quiet," I whispered.

"Oh, we can whisper too," they said.

"No, no," I said quietly, "Don't even talk. *Please*. For five minutes let's just be silent."

"You guys," Emma said sternly, "Mom is about to FREAK out, ok, so be quiet!"

"Alright, we get it!" I heard Katie and Ben mumble. I slowly pulled back onto the road and turned the radio on softly. It didn't take long for Ben to let out an exasperated sigh. He said, "this is SO boring!"

"BEN, you're not supposed to be talking!" Katie yelled.

"Mom, they're talking!" Emma whined.

So much for peace and quiet.

"Mom, will you get a ticket if you drive in your car naked?"-Ben Hughes

Tooth Fairies

The going rate for teeth around these here parts is usually about a dollar. I know, not very much for this inflated marketplace. But the tooth fairy needs to make coffee runs, too, so we do what we have to do. And according to my mom, a quarter was a good haul back in the day.

So we've held firm at a dollar, except for the time Ben took a header to the concrete and ended up loosing his tooth at the tender age of four. That required an extra fifty cents for him and a triple-shot latte for me.

But this last summer, we unknowingly raised the bar for price of teeth. And now, there's no turning back. It was our last day of camping, and the kids were finishing up their breakfast of popcorn and marshmallows (yes, you read that right- we eat pretty healthy while camping). Ben's tooth popped out as he chewed on popcorn kernels and amazingly, he didn't swallow it.

He kept the tooth safe in his pocket until we reached my mom's house. We were having a layover there before continuing our next leg of vacation. I'm pretty sure I can blame what happened next on lack of sleep. Actually, I know I can. For those of you that have been tent camping with kids before, you know that in the course of a night you probably only get two hours of real sleep.

So that night, as I climbed into an actual *bed,* I was not thinking about Ben's tooth at all. I was thinking about sleep- *glorious sleep.* I felt like the bed just wrapped itself around me, and I couldn't keep my eyes open. I smiled as I drifted off to sleep, thinking, "Thank God I don't have to use a flashlight to find the bathroom tonight!"

I woke up in a cold sweat around 2 am. I was confused and didn't know where I was. I let my eyes adjust to the light and then I sat straight up. The tooth! "Oh man!" I thought as I climbed out of the cozy blankets. "Why do they always have to lose their teeth when I'm tired!" I was grumpy and completely unprepared. I tiptoed downstairs, desperate to find some cold, hard cash. I was trying not to wake everyone as I rummaged through my suitcase. I found a dollar bill crumpled up at the bottom of my purse, and felt like I had just hit the jackpot.

On a whim, I decided to throw in a little more. We were on vacation and I guess I was feeling generous. I found forty-eight cents in the pocket of my jeans and fifty-two cents on top of my mom's washing machine (sorry, mom- I'll pay you back.) I crept back upstairs and sure enough, he had remembered to put that little tooth under his pillow. I quickly made the switch and then collapsed back into my deep sleep.

The next morning, Ben was standing over me with a big toothless grin on his face. "Hey mom, I got *four* whole dollars from the tooth fairy last night- that's the most I've ever gotten!"

I tried to rub the sleep out of my eyes. Did he just say four dollars? Inside, I felt very confused. How could this be? I tried to keep my cool and said, "Wow, that's a lot of money!" He smiled and ran off to look at his loot.

I went about my morning until Dave got up. I heard Ben telling him about his big haul. Dave walked into the kitchen looking just as confused. We stared at each other. "Did you put money under his pillow?" Dave asked.

"Yes," I said slowly, "did you?"

A smile spread across his face. "Yep," He said. "I woke up at six in the morning and threw a couple dollars under there. I thought you forgot."

"I thought you forgot!" I said.

Just then Emma ran into the room. She glared straight at us and asked, "How come the tooth fairy gave him so much? I never get that much!"

I busied myself with the coffee maker. When I looked up, she was still glaring at me. I'm guessing she knows who the tooth fairies are. And we'll be paying for our lack of communication for years to come.

"Mom, will you play make-believe with us?" They all asked.

"Sure," I said.

"Ok, you're the mom and we're your kids and you tell us what to do."

"I'm not sure how that's any different than what we're already doing," I said, "Maybe we can work on creating a better make-believe world, ok?"

Thank God for Checkers and Old Ladies

Target is a wonderful store. We used to go there a lot. But that was before the 'incident'. After the 'incident', I would cringe when I saw the big red O sign. It was a couple months before I set foot in one again, and when I did it was *without* kids. Pretty much every store was put on hiatus until I recovered from what happened on that late summer day.

Our outing had started off great. We were in the dog days of summer and I was trying to fill the hot afternoon with something fun. We didn't have an agenda or any sort of shopping list, so after getting our Icees we went to look around. When we got to the shoe department, everyone was in great spirits. Emma went a couple aisles over to look at her size shoes while I scanned the toddler racks for Katie.

"Hey mom," I heard Emma yell, "these high heels over here would totally match the bra you have on today!" Several pairs of eyes glanced in my direction as she proudly held up the leopard print heels. Awesome. It's always fun when total strangers find out what kind of undergarments you have on. This should have been my clue that things were about to take a turn for the worse.

I decided to let Katie pick out some sandals because they were on clearance. She found the perfect pair- sparkly pink with straps. She clutched them to her chest as we wandered around the store for the next half an hour.

She was still smiling as we started making our way to check out. That's when she saw it. A bright purple princess stroller was right there in front of her- like a sunbeam was shining down on it. Her eyes got as big as saucers as she squealed, "It's my most beautiful stroller that I ever wanted!" She ran over to it and promptly set her new shoes down in the seat. She turned to me and declared, "I'm gonna get this stroller for my babies, mommy." (Insert scary, daunting music here.)

I did not answer for five whole seconds as I took some deep breaths. She was not going to like my answer. I walked over and bent down so that we were eye to eye. "We can't buy the stroller, Katie," I said, "it's too expensive and you already got to pick out shoes."

She gripped the handles of the stroller even tighter as she said, "I'm gonna get the shoes *and* the stroller, ok mommy?"

I braced myself. I had lived through many temper tantrums with Emma and Ben, but had yet to see my precious baby girl throw a full- blown hissy fit. But it was coming- oh, was it coming. The sweat beads started to appear on my forehead as I said, "Katie, let go of the stroller and let's go pay for your shoes."

"NO! I want this stroller for my baby!" she screamed.

Well, anyone within a hundred- yard radius heard what happened next. I pried her hands off of the stroller, and that's when my darling little girl decided to throw the biggest temper tantrum I have ever witnessed in my whole life. She threw herself on the floor, wailed, pleaded, kicked and screamed. She shoved the stroller down and banged at the floor with her fist. Her face turned five different shades of red. I glanced over at Emma and Ben, and they looked absolutely horrified.

I knew there would be no reasoning with her. I scooped her up, and made a beeline for the check stand. She kicked and squirmed and YELLED all the way to the front of the store. *Everyone* was watching us, and that's not being over-dramatic. I would be staring too if some lady was speed walking through the store with a screaming toddler under her arm. It didn't help that Katie was yelling, "LET ME GO!" in complete hysteria. That's why I was not surprised to see a security guard standing by the check stands. Maybe it was a coincidence, but I think not.

The line was long. Emma was plugging her ears and Ben had assumed the fetal position at the bottom of the cart. I thought about abandoning ship- I really wanted to. But we needed milk and if I didn't wait in line now, I would have to stop on the way home- and that wasn't going to happen.

She started yelling even louder. The stares were now obvious and I avoided eye contact at all cost. After what felt like an eternity I set the milk down to pay. I pried the sandals out of Katie's little hands and handed them over to the checker. I had to yell over the screaming, but I said, "Here are the shoes she wants. We can't get these because she's throwing a fit. I'm sorry I didn't go put them back myself."

This made Katie cry even harder. The checker took them and then yelled back to me over the noise, "thank you for not giving in. We don't see that happen very often." I tried to smile but the tears were now flowing down *my* face. I gave her three dollars for the milk and then pushed the cart towards the exit. A little old lady caught my arm and said, "you're doing the right thing honey. I know it's hard, but this will pass." I thanked her and barely made it to the parking lot before I burst into tears. Thank God for checkers and old ladies.

Kate screamed all the way home- and for an hour and a half in her room. Then she passed out from exhaustion and slept for two hours. My ears are still ringing to this day. But she didn't get her way. And not only did *she* learn a lesson, her brother and sister saw firsthand that temper tantrums don't ever get you what you want. Sometimes being a responsible adult is very hard. But it's also very worth it.

Planet Earth

One afternoon, Katie wandered into the kitchen and stopped right in front of me. She put her hands on her hips and said, "Mommy, I've been wondering something today."

"What have you been wondering?" I asked her.

"What planet do we live on, anyway?" She asked very seriously.

I got down to her eye level. "We live on planet earth," I said.

"Earth," she said in amazement. "I'm glad I live on earth." Then she walked away.

It's always a good idea to know what planet you live on.

Frozen Yogurt

The kids and I were driving home one afternoon, and you could feel the tension in the air. The day had not been good. It wasn't that any one thing had gone wrong; it was more like a lot of little things. I was distracted with grown-up problems, and the kids were set on driving each other completely crazy. We were all on edge, and had all lost our tempers.

As I waited for the light to turn green, I decided that we needed a distraction. We had been running errands for what seemed like *forever*, and I knew the kids were bored out of their minds. I made a split-second decision to take them out for frozen yogurt. I was 100% sure this would help lift our spirits and get us out of our cranky moods.

When I turned right instead of heading for home, the kids got suspicious. "What are we doing?" Emma asked grumpily. "I thought we were *finally* done with errands."

"I think we need some frozen yogurt!" I declared, trying to sound happy.

"Oh, that's a great idea," Ben said. "Plus, I have to go potty really bad."

As I pulled into a parking space, Ben was already getting unbuckled. "Hey," I said, "slow down! I haven't even stopped the car yet."

"I have to go so bad!" He yelled.

"All the sudden you have to go that bad?" I asked.

"Yes, it's about to come out!" He said in a panicked voice. I sighed and quickly walked over to open his door. I told him to run inside and go to the bathroom, and that we would be coming right behind him. He took off for the door, trying to hold it in at the same time.

The girls and I followed close behind. When I opened the door to the yogurt place, I could see him standing by the bathroom doing *the dance*. He screamed, "Somebody's in the bathroom mom! It's locked!" All eyes were suddenly turned towards us.

I quickly walked over to him and whispered, "I guess you're just going to have to....". I was interrupted by the look of pure relief that passed over his face. This look was followed by instant panic.

"I can't make it stop, mom!" He whispered fiercely. "It just keeps coming!"

I hung my head as a huge pee puddle began to form around his feet. I stood there in disbelief. "I'm so sorry mom," he said. Then he bent over, took off his crocs, and emptied out the pee trapped inside of them. Wonderful.

I didn't dare turn around. I knew most of the people in the tiny shop had just witnessed the whole spectacle. The restroom door opened ten seconds too late. "Watch out for the pee on the floor," I said quietly as the lady walked out. Ben ran into the bathroom and grabbed some paper towels. I couldn't stop the tears from coming as we tried to clean up the mess. Even my fun idea had backfired on me. I needed to go home.

We left in complete silence, and I never made eye contact with anyone. We climbed back in the car and Emma said, "You even ruined frozen yogurt, Ben! This day is just horrible!"

Ben got himself buckled up and then said, "Well, after I get changed we should head over to the other frozen yogurt place- they don't know about me peeing all over the floor."

I sure hope not. But word travels fast in small towns.

Ben: "Hey mom, your bathroom smells really good- did you get new perfume or something?"

Me: "Nope."

Ben: "Oh, I guess my pee just smells really good today."

The Obstacle Course

My sisters and I used to play a game when we were kids that went something like this: One person would set up an obstacle course through the house, and then the other two would have to race through it to see who would be the winner. We were pretty serious about the whole thing, and written instructions were not uncommon. Sometimes it would take over an hour just to set up a course, and another half an hour to explain it to the racers. Yeah, we were pretty hard- core.

On one particular afternoon, it was my turn to come up with something amazing. While my sisters watched Rainbow Brite in the living room, I was busy creating the ultimate obstacle course. It was going to be legendary. I couldn't wait for them to run through it.

Finally, everything was ready. They stood in front of me waiting for instructions. I handed them a little map of the course, and then told them there was a catch. This time, they had to run through the obstacle course *together-* working as a team. I seriously thought this was a genius idea, and couldn't believe we hadn't thought of it before.

They looked confused. To help them understand, I tied them together with a big scrunchie (they were little, so it just slipped right over their heads.) I swear to you that NO red flags were going off in my mind at all. But then again, I was all of ten years old and didn't really think *anything* through.

I started the timer and off they went. It was hilarious seeing them try to run up and down hallways, crawl over laundry baskets, and walk down stairs. They were laughing, too, and not making good time at all. I was following behind them as they made their way into the final stretch. I watched as they climbed up the side of the bunk bed and sat on the edge.

Now, the bunk beds were always a part of our obstacle course- they were the only thing high enough to add some sort of suspense to the game. But no one had ever been tied together. I will admit, some sort of alarm sounded very deep inside of my brain as I waited for them to jump. But I didn't have the chance to act on it. Right before my eyes, I watched my littlest sister jump from the top of the bunk bed. The problem was, my other sister did *not* jump. This was not good- not good at all.

One was temporarily suspended in mid- air, and then milliseconds later the other was catapulted off the edge. It was pretty freaky. Thank God they didn't land on each other, but some damage had been done. Their frantic screams quickly brought my mom running full speed from downstairs. She scanned the scene in disbelief and assessed the damage. I stood there in shock, still not quite understanding that the whole thing was my fault.

"Why are they tied together?" My mom yelled over all the crying. "And why did they jump off the bed?"

All of the sudden I knew that this did not look good for me. "It was part of the game," I whispered.

"Did you tie them together?" She asked. I suddenly felt nauseous. I nodded. "Go to your room while I make sure they're ok!"

I went in my room and cried. I couldn't believe that I almost killed them- my best friends and sisters. As the minutes ticked by, I just knew that they were headed to the hospital with broken legs and arms. My life was over.

My mom came in awhile later. She told me they were ok, thank God, and only had some cuts and bruises. "What were you thinking?" She asked me.

"I have no idea!" I answered tearfully. "But I swear, I wasn't trying to kill them, I promise!"

She laughed. "I know that. You have to use some more common sense, though, ok?"

"Next time we play, I won't tie them together," I said.

"No, no one can play that game anymore-ever," she said seriously. And I think we'll take the bunk beds down, too."

My sisters eventually forgave me for their near-death experience. At least, I think they did. But I am reminded of it *all the time.* When Emma climbs ten feet up a tree and then can't get down, I remember the bunk beds. When Ben pulls out all of our carrots before they've even grown an inch, I remember the obstacle course. And when Katie cuts her own bangs, I remember that fateful day. Kids do stupid stuff. They don't think everything through. And I try to be patient. Because my mom was patient with me- a *lot.*

Me: "What was your most favorite part of camping?"

Ben: "Definitely exploring in the woods."

Me: "Okay, so what was your least favorite part?"

Ben: (without hesitation) "When I had to stop exploring to go poop."

What's that on Your Face?

I was standing in the checkout line at Fred Meyer on a busy Friday afternoon. People were lined up behind me, waiting as the checker rang up our groceries. Katie was sitting on the floor at my feet, complaining that she was hungry. Ben was standing near the front of the basket singing "I just want to go home now" to the tune of Twinkle Twinkle Little Star. Emma had been talking non-stop about the characters she likes on Jessie, how much she liked learning about igneous rocks and why Hershey's was her favorite kind of chocolate.

I was in survival mode, trying desperately to concentrate and keep the smile pasted on my face until we got to the car. The day had been *LONG*. I was about to pull my wallet out of my purse when Emma gasped and said, "Mom! You have a huge red spot on your nose! It's really big- I can't believe I haven't noticed it today."

I'm pretty sure I saw at least six pairs of eyes turn in my direction and stare right at my nose. It was like the scene out of a bad movie- when all the background noise fades out, and the camera lens zooms in on the main character's face for a good close-up.

I tried to keep my cool. "Oh, I don't know," I said, "I'll have to look at it in the car, ok?"

"But it looks like it hurts, what do you think it is? A huge bug bite?" Emma was definitely concerned, and talking in a not so quiet voice. I gave her a heated stare.

"It's not a bug bite- it's *FINE*," I whispered, feeling my face turn four shades of red. By now everyone was averting their eyes and looking very uncomfortable. I don't blame them.

She started to pick up on my freaky mom voice but it was too late. And then, at that moment, she realized what it was- and because common sense had already flown the coop, she covered her mouth and yelled, "Oh, it's a big zit! Sorry mom!"

So was I- and so was the checker who had lots of them too. I swiped my card as fast as I could and avoided eye contact. When he handed me the receipt and said the standard, "Have a nice day, ma'am," I couldn't help but shoot him the evil eye too.

"Well," he said sympathetically, "at least it's almost over, right?"

That was true. So, I pushed my cart filled with groceries, three whiney kids, and my big huge ZIT right out of the store.

Car Safety and Karaoke

When Emma was three this is how we would play Barbie's: First she would dress them perfectly, then she would pick out two to ride in the Barbie car. She would place them in the car very carefully, making sure each one was buckled in and all the doors were doors closed. The other Barbie's she was playing with would have to wait in line for the car to come back- because safety always comes first, of course.

The Barbie's would dance around in their dresses, and then change into their swimsuits for a trip to the Water Park. They all had the right clothes for the right occasion, and they always arrived safely at their destination.

Now that Katie is three, I get to experience playing with Barbie's in a whole new way. This is how Katie plays with them: She stuffs about twelve Barbie dolls into a car, some on their heads and some with limbs sticking out of the doors. There is absolutely no buckling up going on at all. As she pushes them down the hallway she screams, "Hang on girls or you'll fly out!" She usually loses one or two on the sharp curve into the kitchen. She just keeps going, yelling over her shoulder, "We'll pick you up next time!"

When they arrive at the ball, some are in swimming suits, some are in gowns, and some are just plain naked. Their hair is crazy and none of them have shoes. Instead of dancing elegantly, they take turns singing karaoke- they really like to sing "Jesus Loves Me" and "The Star Spangled Banner." When they are done singing, she piles them in the car, races back down the hallway and dumps them on the bed. Sadly, some never make it back to the room.

I'm a little concerned on many levels. Obviously she is not interested in following the rules of the road. Not to mention the fact that she takes corners so fast that Skipper flies out and hit's the wall. But mostly I'm concerned about the Barbie's singing Karaoke naked to Sunday school songs. I'm very thankful that high school is still twelve years away. And I've decided that when Katie goes to college she's going to move in with Emma for as long as possible.

"Hey Mom, I just decided that instead of making a gingerbread *house* this year I'm going to make a gingerbread *gun*- it'll be way cooler." -Ben Hughes

Cops and Robbers

One night Katie and Ben decided to play cops and robbers. Every five minutes Katie would run shrieking through the house with Ben hot on her heels. Once apprehended, she was taken to the 'jail' to await sentencing. They both thought the whole thing was hilarious, and I was so happy they were entertaining themselves.

I was helping Emma with some homework and after a few minutes I realized Katie had not come shrieking through the kitchen in awhile. Just when Dave was about to go investigate, Ben came walking around the corner. "I have some bad news," he said with a grim look on his face, "Kate's locked in my jail."

I played along with the game and said dramatically, "Oh, no! That's just *HORRIBLE*!" Then I smiled and turned back to Emma's spelling list.

"No, I'm serious, mom," he said, "I can't get the door open. I think she's stuck in there forever."

"How'd she lock the door?" Dave asked as he headed down the hallway.

"Well, I actually locked it and then shut the door. I just wasn't using my brain I guess," he said.

When we got to the door, I knocked on it and asked, "Kate, are you ok in there, honey?"

Lots of giggling followed. And then she knocked back and said, "Hi mommy!"

Dave asked her if she could try and unlock the door, but she was clueless and couldn't figure it out. "Don't worry Katie, daddy will get you out," Emma yelled in a motherly voice. Ben seemed very excited that we might have to bust down the door. Apparently he had already forgotten that he was in big trouble.

While Dave tried to open the door from inside, I went around the house to see if our bedroom window was unlocked. I was starting to get worried that she might be scared or nervous. I couldn't have been more wrong. There she was, bouncing on our bed, throwing pillows, and going through my jewelry box. She was also having fun turning the lights on, then off, then on again. She didn't have a care in the world.

By the time we got the door open, she had changed the alarms on our clock, emptied our nightstands, and piled the pillows up to make a tower. I don't think she ever even realized she was actually locked up. Either that or she genuinely enjoys the solitude of prison.

Whatever the case, Ben was very relieved to see her set free from her imprisonment. That meant he wasn't in as *much* trouble as he had been before. From this moment on, I was pretty certain we would never be leaving the two of them home alone together- ever.

Telescope

I opened the door to the bathroom and was greeted by a massive pile of toilet paper- just an hour before I had put a fresh roll on, so I knew something was amiss. The toilet paper roller was laying in the sink, which further solidified my case- someone very short and mischievous had just been in there.

"Katie, why is there a mountain of toilet paper in here?" I yelled.

She came running around the corner. "Oh, hi," she said with a smile.

"Hi," I said pointing at the empty roller, "why is that roller in the sink and what happened to all the toilet paper?"

"I needed a telescope for my game," she said matter-of-factly.

Of course she did. "What are we going to do with all of that now?" I asked as I kicked at the mound with my foot.

"We can still use it, mom, you just have to bend over and get it, like this." She bent over and demonstrated how to pick it up.

She's such a problem solver.

The Trip that shall not be Named

We waited nine years to take our kids to Disneyland. I had been itching to go since they were in diapers, but my more level- headed husband thought we should wait. He wasn't really sold on the idea of Disneyland anyway, and the thought of standing in long lines with toddlers kept him up at night. So, we waited.

At first it was easy, because our kids didn't know it existed at all. But when they started grade school, they realized that there was a place on earth dubbed 'The Happiest'. At least every other week they would come home and say, "Mom, so and so just got back from

Disneyland! She said it was *awesome*! When is it going to be our turn to go?"

When Katie turned three, Dave could no longer hold me at bay. Emma was in third grade and Ben was in Kindergarten- the perfect age. It was time for us to introduce them to some Disney magic, and I could hardly wait. It was going to be the trip of a lifetime, and we were ready to make some wonderful family memories.

We planned everything perfectly. We bought our tickets. We found the perfect hotel. We researched stroller rentals, show times, height requirements for rides, restaurants, and we made sure to pack weather appropriate clothes. We were going to be prepared for anything and everything, so that our trip would go as smooth as possible.

We arrived at Disneyland full of excitement and anticipation. But life was about to throw us a gigantic curveball that none of us ever expected. Less than twenty-two hours after we touched down in Anaheim, we got the Stomach Flu- *every single one of us.* Nothing could have prepared us for that.

Our first morning there, Ben whispered four little words that instantly changed our dream vacation into a nightmare: "My mouth feels funny." Then he proceeded to throw up over and over and *over.*

It's awful to be away from home when you're sick. It's even worse when five people are sick in a small hotel room. But being *across the street* from Disneyland when you have the flu? That's just torture, plain and simple. No one even wanted to open the shades. Nothing good was going to come from looking at a roller coaster we couldn't even go on.

Our room was disgusting within five hours. We were putting in calls for new sheets at least twice a day. The housekeeping staff definitely deserved a medal of bravery for cleaning our room every day. The smell was awful. We just didn't have anywhere to go, and we had none of the comforts of home.

The first two days we simply tried to stay alive. I know that sounds dramatic, but that's exactly how it felt. We were not prepared for something of this magnitude. Instead of spending our money on Mickey ears, T-shirts and Princess crowns, we spent most of it at the convenience store across the street. We spent a fortune on Tylenol, orange juice, ginger ale, saltines and LOTS of paper towels.

After two days of not leaving the hotel room, Dave and I knew we had to come up with a plan. We decided to tag-team with the kids. One of us would stay at the hotel with whoever was barfing, and the other would attempt to take a kid to the park. And then we would just pray that we could make it to the main gate before we needed a bathroom- yes, it was THAT bad. I'm pretty sure I could tell you exactly where every bathroom is and how long it takes to walk there.

We only got a couple of days at Disneyland as a family, but even those are very blurry. No one really wanted to ride anything, and even cotton candy was left untouched. I can count on my fingers how many pictures we took, and no one could walk more than a few minutes without getting tired. We were scared to stand in any type of line. We would buy fifty dollars worth of food and then sit and stare at it. No one could choke it down. Even the wonderful Disney characters couldn't make the kids smile.

I was too exhausted to be mad. That would come later. I was just very, very sad. It was hard to see my kids disappointed. For weeks they had been excited to watch the fireworks show from Main Street. Instead, they sat at our tiny hotel room window, clutching bowls to their chests, trying to see them in the distance.

One afternoon I took Ben and Emma to California Adventure. They took turns riding in a stroller as we slowly walked around. Ben got hungry, so I bought him an $8 hotdog. Half an hour later, we realized that we left it on the condiment table. The thought of backtracking for five minutes drained the life-blood right out me, so I bought him another $8 hotdog at the closest stand. He promptly dropped that one on the ground after a few bites. I asked him if those three bites were worth $16. He said, "Yes". That's how tired and pathetic we were.

We somehow survived. I almost kissed out taxi driver when he came to pick us up. No one had been spared. The flu had made its way through us all, hitting Katie on the very last day. Dave and I both lost over six pounds and most of our sanity. Not much was said on our flights home. We were simply too exhausted to talk anymore.

The weeks following were really hard. To say we were disappointed would be a major understatement. I was so mad, and couldn't comprehend why this would have happened. We waited so long to go on this trip. We saved up a lot of money. We had been excited to get a break from our hectic life.

Even as I write this, I still don't understand. But I'm not mad anymore. We can't control every situation, and unfortunately, life doesn't always go the way we want. God is in control, and I put my faith and trust in that. He has an ultimate plan for our lives, and somehow our experience at Disneyland needed to happen the way it did.

It took a few months, but slowly Dave and I started to see some things differently. We realized that even though the trip was very disappointing, we did learn a few things. In a weird sort of way, this experience strengthened us as parents. We only had each other to lean on. We had to be extremely patient with each other in a very frustrating circumstance.

We also came together as a family, and we learned that we *are* stronger than we think. It was a hard life lesson for our kids to learn: Life is not always perfect. You will be disappointed. You will feel discouraged. You will want to scream and shout, "It's just not fair!" at the top of your lungs. You will feel like giving up.

But we can't give up. There's so much more to life than Disneyland. We have to pick ourselves up and let it go. It's the people in our lives that make all the difference. When we fix our eyes on what matters most, these hang-ups of life won't get us down. If we can find even a smidgen of joy in the worst of circumstances, we will make it out ok.

"When you walk by your Christmas tree and see stray pieces of string cheese, dirty socks, crusty noodles and a phone cord draping the branches, it's probably time to take it down."-Nikki Hughes

You Want to Be Friends?

Katie made a new friend at the library one day. I watched from the other side of the room as a little boy walked up to her and said, "You want to be friends and read together?"

She said "Sure!" and they sat down to look at a book about pumpkins. About five minutes later she came running up to me and said, "Mommy, I have to go to the bathroom so bad!"

"Ok, let's go," I said as I put down my magazine.

She ran back over to the little boy and knelt down beside him. She told him very seriously, "I have to go poop right now but when I come back we can still be friends."

He looked at her and said, "That's fine."

I decided that the next time I met someone new, I would skip the boring pleasantries. I would just tell them I have to go poop but still want to be friends. It worked pretty well for Katie.

Cooking Skills

Dave turned on the oven to bake some rolls. As it pre-heated, there was a strong burned odor that filled the whole house. Our oven obviously needed to be cleaned. After a few minutes the kids wandered in to investigate. Emma said, "Something smells like burnt rubber! It's grossing me out!"

Katie looked at her and said, "I bet mommy's making her special chicken for dinner again."

Toots

We had a packed car on the way to church one night. Five girls and one boy filled the backseats, and no one could get a word in edgewise. With three friends in the car, there is never a shortage of things to talk about. Suddenly, I heard Ben shout over the noise, "Hey mom, you might want to crack the window because I just farted."

I glanced back to see him sitting calmly with his hands behind his head and a big smile on his face. Emma and her friends began to squeal and gag from the backseat. Emma yelled, "Ben, that's so gross!" And then she turned to her friends and said, "He has THE worst toots ever!" They all giggled while plugging their noses.

He was still smiling, very proud of himself for grossing them out. "By the way," he said, "I have lots more toots coming, so you better just leave it cracked the whole way to church." He looked behind him to see their reaction. He wasn't disappointed. More giggling, gagging and whispering followed.

I went ahead and rolled it down the whole way. I seriously hope he comes up with a different strategy to impress girls, at least by the time he's fifteen.

"I'm becoming too grown-up to eat cookie dough ice cream. I think I'm old enough to eat peppermint now that I'm in third grade."-Emma Hughes

Hitchhiking

I hitchhiked once. There, I said it. And to this day, I still think my mom has nightmares about it. Hitchhiking definitely holds a place on the top five stupidest things I've ever done in my whole life. Whenever someone brings up the story (usually one of my dear sisters), my mom has to physically leave the room. I'm pretty sure this incident caused most of the gray hairs that now reside on her head.

I was twenty-three and absolutely head-over-heels in love with a strapping State Trooper. I clearly wasn't thinking straight. In fact, the whole reason I resorted to hitchhiking in the first place was because of his handsome face. Because I missed him so much when we were apart, I had put his picture on the console of my car, right behind the steering wheel. That way I could glance down at him whenever I wanted.

The problem was, his picture totally covered my fuel gauge. I mean, really, who needs to know how much gas they have in their car when they are *completely* in love? I do, apparently. But I guess I was under the impression that all you needed was love.

I was driving down the interstate, on the way to meet (you guessed it) my *mom*. I was singing with the radio at the top of my lungs when I felt my car do a little jolt. Then, it made some funny noises. And finally, it started slowing down. I pulled over to the side of the road and sat there. I had no idea what to do. I was furious with my car, and even banged the steering wheel with my hand. I thought for sure it had overheated or the engine had given out.

I got out and popped the hood. No smoke-everything seemed fine. I checked the oil and miraculously there was some still in it. So, I got back in the car and contemplated what might be wrong. I tried starting it again-nothing. "Why won't you start?" I yelled. I glanced down at Dave's picture, and then, a light bulb appeared right over my head. "Oh, man!" I screamed as I grabbed his picture off the dashboard. My gas was at zero. I felt like an idiot.

I knew my mom was waiting for me forty miles down the freeway, but I had no way of getting a hold of her. Looking back, I realize that I should have put my hazards on and waited for a police officer to pass by. But, I was young and invincible, and could solve this problem all by myself. I grabbed my purse, Dave's picture, and my keys. I locked the car and started walking down the freeway. My first instinct was to walk to the nearest exit. But I couldn't even see one as far as the eye could see.

At that point I proceeded to throw all my common sense to the wind. I stuck my thumb out. It only took about two minutes for a car to stop- a car with three gentlemen inside. I explained the situation, and they said they would take me to the nearest exit. Even as I type this, my stomach is knotting up. I have my own girls now, and can't imagine them climbing into a car with total strangers. Sadly, we live in a world where this is just not safe at all.

They were true to their word, and actually very nice. But this was only by the grace of God. I know that now. At the gas station, I walked over to a pay phone. Then I hung my head. I had absolutely no quarters. So then, I had to go beg for money. Yes, all in one day I had become a hitchhiker and a panhandler. You can see why mom has trouble reminiscing about the whole thing.

A nice old lady gave me a couple quarters. When my mom picked up on the other end, she said, "Hey, when will you be here?"

I paused. I was suddenly more scared than I had been while stranded on the freeway. How was I supposed to rationalize any of this? She was going to be so mad. I decided to just rip the Band-Aid right off. As fast as I could, I said, "I ran out of gas on interstate five. I hitchhiked to the nearest exit and then begged for money so I could call you. I'm fine, I just need you to come get me and buy a gas can and take me back to my car." Whew. That didn't sound so bad, right?

Wrong. A few seconds of silence proceeded the inevitable. "You what?" She screamed into the phone. "You hitchhiked! What on earth were you thinking! You could have been killed!" I let her yell and cry, because I seriously deserved it. The more she talked, the more everything seemed to come crashing down around me. I suddenly felt myself shaking, and couldn't believe I had just done what I did. The more I tried to rationalize the situation, the worse it got.

When she pulled up to the convenience store thirty minutes later, I expected more yelling. But the car was barely in park when she jumped out and threw her arms around me. She hugged me so tight I could barely breathe. "Don't you *ever* do that again," she whispered through her tears.

Later, as we finished putting gas in my car, she asked, "How on earth did you manage to run out of gas on the freeway?"

"It's all Dave's fault," I said. "His face was in the way." I was trying to joke around, but she didn't crack a smile. I guess it was way too soon to laugh about the whole thing.

Katie yelled from the other room, "Mom, I want some juice!"

I peeked around the corner and said, "Is that how we ask for juice?"

She paused and then said, "Oh. Sorry. I want some juice right now!"

Check Out Those Booties!

We took a spur-of-the-moment trip to Astoria, Oregon one weekend. It was very good for the soul to get away even for just a couple days. The kids were SO excited. They even made up a song on the way that went something like this - "Astoria, Astoria, the place where all your dreams come true." They sang it over and over and OVER. Either they are easy to please or we just don't get out that much.

We stayed overnight at a hotel overlooking the Columbia River. The kids were glued to the window whenever we were in the room; watching the boats, sea lions, and runners who were exercising on the walking trail. Ben had brought his binoculars and basically stood perfectly still staring out of those things the whole time. He would make a good lighthouse keeper or undercover spy someday.

In the morning as we were packing up, Ben was still standing there at his post, binoculars glued to his eyes. All of the sudden he said excitedly "check out that great booty out there!" We all turned to look at him. Did he just say booty?

Dave walked over with a look of confusion on his face. "What did you say?" He asked Ben.

"I see some awesome booties out the window!" Ben exclaimed again, never averting his gaze. I was prepping myself for an interesting conversation about the female body. Dave wasn't sure what to expect when he looked out the window, but much to his relief, there were no beautiful women in sight. Upon closer inspection, he realized Ben was staring out into the river.

"What do you see again?" Dave asked.

"I see booties," he replied, "floating out there on the water- green ones!"

Ah. Mystery solved. The boy saw Buoys- not *booties*.

I let out a big sigh of relief. I had not raised a peeping tom after all, just a boy that loved him some nautical excitement.

"Thank you God that I'm so pretty."-Katie Hughes

Nail Polish

Katie wanted me to paint her nails. So, I sat her on the kitchen counter and she explained how she wanted them painted- in a pattern of green and pink. I got to work. The problem was that she kept trying to grab the nail polish bottles and do it herself. After a few warnings I said, again, "Don't touch those- I've already told you three times!"

"But I want to help," she said.

"I know, but if you knock over one of these bottles I'm going to be very frustrated. It's so hard to clean up." I took a deep breath and continued painting.

Just then the timer beeped on the oven. I turned to look at it and knocked over the bottle of green polish. It flew off the counter and splattered all over the floor. I stood there in shock. Katie's jaw dropped and her eyes got wide.

"Well, I guess you can be frustrated at yourself now, mommy," she said.

A Day in the Garage

"I'm going out in the garage to work on my knife," Dave told me one morning. He sounded completely serious and looked like he was on a mission to actually accomplish something. God bless him and his optimistic thoughts. I just smiled and said, "Have fun!" as he headed out to his workbench.

See, if your kids are anything like ours, they gravitate towards whatever is cooler than what they're already doing. I knew it was only a matter of time that their little noses would smell something going on in the garage.

It took exactly five minutes. At the first sound of a power tool, they dropped their crayons and made a beeline for the garage. Before the door shut behind them I could already hear the questions being shouted above the noise of the drill: "Whatcha doing dad?", "Can I help, dad?", "I want to build something too!"

I thought about rescuing him- for about half a second. Then I realized how quiet the house suddenly was, and I decided I should take advantage of it. I took a long hot shower, folded some laundry and even got to sit down at the computer for a few minutes.

After half an hour I decided to go out and check on everyone. I opened the door to the garage and held my breath. His knife sat untouched on the workbench. Instead, he was busy running back and forth between kid projects. He was helping Emma build a birdhouse out of Popsicle sticks, overseeing Ben hammer nails into a wooden sign, and opening paint bottles for Katie.

They had got to him. Broke him down one question at a time. I quickly slipped back into the house before anyone could see me. I grabbed the car keys and tried to make a break for it. As I passed by the flurry of activity I happily shouted, "I'll bring back lunch for all of you hardworkers!" Dave gave me a look that just screamed, "Please God don't let her leave me here with all of them."

He put on a brave face and wiped the sweat from his brow. "Ok, you'll be back *soon*, right?" He asked. I just smiled.

In the end the kids were ecstatic. One birdhouse was constructed. A jewelry box was spray painted and covered in stickers. A wooded sign was sawed and written on. Scrap pieces of wood covered the garage floor and two kids were coated in paint and glue.

And in the end one dad was exhausted. And one knife still sat undone. But they were together all day, and the sweat was worth it. That night as I tucked the kids into bed, they all said that working in the garage with their dad was the best part of the day. Just before Katie fell asleep, she said, "My dad can fix anything. He's the best."

"I don't want Katie to sit by me! She's bossy and smelly and annoying. But she's also cute so maybe it's ok." - Ben Hughes

The Amusement Park

One day last summer we surprised the kids with a day at the amusement park. I knew the kids were going to have a total blast. And for some reason, I am really good at going into complete denial about reality, so I figured Dave and I would have a great time too.

When we pulled into the parking lot the kids let out squeals of delight and I instantly felt severely nauseous. *Every single ride* was spinning. I glanced sideways at Dave and he had the same look on his face that I had- a strange mix of regret, panic, and resolve. We had come this far and made too many promises; we could not turn back now.

We headed to buy wristbands that would guarantee us endless rides and ultimately be our dire fate. The minute the kids got their bracelets the day became a blur: "Go on the scrambler with me mom!", "How about the carousel!", "Oh, look, an upside down roller coaster!" Dave and I were both about to upchuck after the first half an hour. But that didn't stop us- we were determined not to act like we were getting *old!*

As if the rides weren't enough crazy for us, we also decided to attempt roller-skating as a family. This proved to be interesting. Katie moved at a snail's pace and I'm pretty sure only took one loop around the rink the entire hour we were there. Ben had no coordination whatsoever. He flailed around like a fish out of water. He never made it around the rink. Well, unless you count the loop he made while hanging on to Dave for dear life.

Emma got the hang of it pretty fast- luckily she got her daddy's coordination.

And that leaves me. I was still feeling pretty nauseous as I strapped on the skates, and my feet hurt like nobody's business by my second lap. The sweat was pouring down my forehead as I tried to remain upright and keep Katie from falling and cracking her head open.

But after an hour, I was starting to loosen up. I was feeling pretty good, getting my skating groove back on. The kids had worn out by then and were sitting behind the wall with Dave. I was ready to feel like a kid again. "I'm gonna go a few laps by myself!" I yelled over to them. They just stared at me like I was crazy.

I felt free without a kid clinging onto me, and I picked up my speed. I felt transported back in time, to the dog days of summer in the late 80's when my sisters and I would skate to the hokey-pokey. As I circled the rink I could almost hear songs like "Groovy Kind of Love" and "I've had the Time of My Life". I was thinking to myself, "Dang, I still got it. I am rocking this right now!"

I was going pretty fast. At least I felt like it. I had gotten a little cocky, going close to the wall and giving my family high-fives as I raced by. I could tell they were impressed, but it's pretty easy to impress the under nine crowd. As I rounded a curve, the announcement came on and said, "Everyone please clear the rink and make your way to the nearest exit- open skate is over."

I don't know what happened next. I'm pretty sure I panicked. As God is my witness I tried to slow down. I tried to turn towards an exit. I tried to stop the inevitable. But right there in front of my family and many other witnesses, I crashed and burned hard. It wasn't pretty. In the split second before I hit, I actually thought, "How can I land in a way that I break the least amount of bones?" My legs went separate ways, my sunglasses went flying and my knee took a direct hit. I do remember hearing some sort of collective gasp coming from the crowd of onlookers.

The funny thing about falling on roller skates is that you have to get up again- and that ain't pretty. I chose to sort of belly crawl across the floor. Most people had a look of pity. Some even showed a little concern. But my family? They were laughing. Yep, Ben was practically doubled over he was laughing so hard. Dave tried to show some concern, but couldn't hide his smile. "Man, you should have seen your face right before you hit!" He said.

I was ready to take my humiliated self home and ice my knee, but first I had to ride some more spinny rides and eat some greasy curly fries. It was all about the experience.

Six hours later we piled back into the car and headed home. Dave and I both felt like we had the flu. My knee was throbbing. The car seemed like it was spinning on it's own. We drove home in silence.

"We're not eighteen anymore," I whispered as I grabbed his hand. He nodded. No other words were necessary.

Hookers

The kids and I ventured out to the store on Black Friday to check out the sales. We were walking through the storage aisle when Ben suddenly yelled out, "Hey mom, wouldn't it be funny if I came to Black Friday just so I could buy a bunch of hookers? They're so cheap!"

I looked up to see that he was pointing to a big rack of coat hangers. But it still drew quite a few stares from our fellow shoppers.

Yep, that's my kid. I claim him most of the time.

Toy Trouble

Katie was refusing to pick up toys. She was using every excuse in the book. Her tummy hurt, she had a hangnail, she was so thirsty, I was mean, she was too tired, she needed to go potty, she needed help, and her head was sore. Too bad for her, because I've heard every excuse in the book and don't fall for any of that these days. I guess that's what she gets for being the third kid.

I finally sat her on my lap, looked her in the eyes and said, "I'm going to go get a garbage bag now and throw away your toys, because it seems like you don't care enough about them to pick them up."

I thought this would scare her straight. But instead, she got a big smile on her face and said, "That's ok, I've been wanting to get new toys anyway!" Lord have mercy.

I'll Just Eat Later

I was making lunch as quickly as I could. The kids had been sitting at the table staring at me for ten minutes, so I knew they were hungry. God forbid we go two hours without eating anything. So, I set the plates down on the table, we said a quick prayer and then they all dug in.

I'm not quite sure what happened to me next. I just got totally grossed out. I suddenly felt like I was living with a bunch of cave people, or monkeys that throw banana peels at each other and pick bugs off each other's backs. It was like the scene out of Bill and Ted's Excellent Adventure when the Mongolian emperor digs into the huge drumstick, and continues barking orders while meat sprays out of his mouth.

I sat there and watched. That's all I could do. I watched as Emma's egg salad slid down her arm and got caught on her sleeve. Then she flicked it off on the table. Katie's ham slipped out of her sandwich and fell on the floor. She quickly scooped it up, squeezed it in her little fist, and stuffed it back in her mouth. Ben was munching on chips like a bunny rabbit and the pile of crumbs was growing around his chair.

As the three of them sat there laughing and slurping up buttered noodles with their bare hands, I glanced to the other end of the table at Dave. My only hope for sanity lay with him. And sure enough, his food sat untouched as *he* took in the crazy scene.

He offered me a smile. I smiled back and told myself, "Someday we will have a nice relaxing meal complete with candlelight and soft music- I just know it. Maybe we'll sit overlooking the beach and eat lobster and actually have a nice conversa…."

Before I could finish my daydream Katie shoved her chair away from the table and announced, "I'm going poop but I'll be right back. Come wipe me, ok, mom?"

Sure. And I think I'll just finish eating later.

"Guess what, Mom? I had no idea that Dad is a genius, but he is!"- Emma Hughes

Bored

I heard a commotion coming from Katie's bedroom. I went to investigate and there she was dumping all of her drawers out onto the floor. Her books were off of her bookshelf and stuffed animals were scattered everywhere.

"Whatcha doin?" I asked.

She let out a big sigh and sat down in the middle of the mess. "I'm so bored, mommy. I think we need to get out of this house."

"Ok, but why is everything dumped out in here?" I was confused.

"It was the only thing to do while you were on the phone," she said dramatically.

"But now you have to clean it up before we can go anywhere," I told her.

She looked stunned. She growled in frustration and yelled, "I AM SO MAD AT MYSELF RIGHT NOW!"

Being a Grown-up is Overrated

I was awakened to the phone ringing at five in the morning. I fumbled around for the light switch and quickly picked it up. An automated voice on the other end said, "Due to a legitimate terror threat, please do not send your child to school today. The authorities are investigating and we will be giving updates throughout the day."

I hung up and couldn't fall back asleep. I suddenly felt like I lived in a world I did not understand- a world that scared me. I couldn't shake the feeling all day. The kids were enjoying their extra day off, but I was pretty shaken. That afternoon, Dave had to leave for work. He had been working some swing shifts, so our schedule was a little off. Usually his crazy work schedule didn't bother me, but that night I just didn't want him to go. I wanted us to be together, for my own sanity.

After he left, my plan was to put the kids to bed and get some things done around the house. But as the minutes ticked by, I realized that I just didn't want to be alone. I pondered this for awhile- the responsible adult inside of me was screaming "PUT THEM TO BED WHILE YOU HAVE THE CHANCE!" But the little girl inside me was longing for some company, longing to just have some FUN, and longing to not be worried about the world and all it's problems for just a little while.

The girl won. At 7:30 we piled in the car and drove to get ice cream cones. We drove with the windows down and talked about our favorite memories of the summer. We talked about how even though sometimes the world seems scary, we know that God is always in control. We talked about jellyfish, traveling to Mars, how to become a ventriloquist, and how much money it would take to buy a kindle. We laughed and it was perfect.

When we got back home I made them a deal. I would let them stay up and watch America's Got Talent (their favorite show at the time), but only if they quickly cleaned their rooms, brushed their teeth and fed the animals. They looked a little shocked by this, but quickly said yes. A few minutes later I heard them whispering in the bathroom:

Emma: "I think mom forgot it was a school night. Do you think she's confused?"

Ben: "I think she forgot. Are you gonna say anything?"

Emma: "No way. Are you?"

Ben: "Nope."

Emma: "Do you think Katie will tell her?"

Ben: "Katie doesn't even know what day it is."

Emma: "This is SO awesome! Oh, be quiet, I think she's coming..."

We watched the whole show cuddled up together with lots of blankets and pillows. They didn't fall asleep till 10:30, but I didn't regret one single minute of it. After a tough day filled with uncertainty, it felt really good to put my kids to bed with smiles on all our faces. I told myself that I would be more responsible tomorrow, but sometimes being a grown-up is over-rated.

Picture Day

It was picture day at school. I had woken the kids up extra early to make sure they were ready. I took Ben into his room to pick out an outfit to wear. He opened his closet and pointed to the first shirt he saw. "That one's fine," he said, and then he ran out of the room. So, I picked out a NICE shirt and that was that.

Then I asked Emma if she had chosen her picture day outfit. She had been brainstorming for two weeks already, so I assumed she had somewhat of an idea. "Not yet, mom!" she said with frustration. She was standing in front of her closet with a towel wrapped around her hair.

Fifteen minutes later I went back to check on her-clothes were strewn everywhere. "Have we narrowed it down yet?" I asked with a smile. She fell back on her bed with a huge dramatic sigh and said, "This is the biggest decision of my entire life! This picture is going to be hanging on the wall for a whole YEAR, mom!" I stared at her for a few seconds. Then I slowly backed out of the room and closed the door behind me.

I decided to keep my distance until the decision had been made. It was much safer that way.

What's an Ironing Board?

I was cleaning out the laundry room. I was on a mission to finally find every single missing sock in our house. To do this, I had to move things around and look in every crack and cranny. I grabbed the ironing board from behind the washing machine and carried it out into the hall. Katie was coming in the other direction, and she stopped cold in her tracks. Her eyes got as wide as saucers and she said, "I didn't know you had your own surfboard, mommy!"

Apparently I had not ironed one single piece of clothing since the day she was born.

Monday Mornings

I thought my Monday morning was going pretty good. Kids were up and seemed rested. Lunches were packed with time to spare. I even paid a couple bills and did a load of laundry. I was rocking it.

My first clue that all chaos was about to break loose came at exactly 8:13. Ben was changing into his school clothes and couldn't get his pajama top off. I helped him and then said, "Wow, I think you're in a growth spurt. This shirt is getting way too small."

He instantly broke down in tears, gripping the pajamas close to his chest. "This is my favorite shirt in the whole world, and I'm gonna wear it until I'm eighty years old," he sobbed.

As I tried to process this interesting new development, Emma came huffing into the room with a towel still wrapped around her head. "I have NOTHING to wear!" she exclaimed and then turned and stomped off. Katie then proceeded to spill her orange juice all over the couch.

I took a deep breath. This couldn't be happening. I was loosing control faster than a runaway train. At 8:50am I yelled, "We're leaving in five minutes!"

This was met with groans and stomping of feet. I headed out to the car to buckle Katie in and found a puddle of water on the backseat. Someone had left a water bottle upside down. I reached into the seat pocket to get some napkins and felt something sticky. At the bottom of the pocket was crushed up cheese, crackers and an old apple core. Awesome.

I felt myself loosing my cool. "We're leaving!" I yelled with absolutely NO patience whatsoever. Ben came running outside and said, "I have library today and I can't find my book!" I hung my head. I slowly calculated how many more hours until bedtime. Eleven. I gritted my teeth.

I spent three minutes looking for the book to no avail. He would have to go without it. He climbed into the car in tears. Emma got in at the very last minute. I brought up the crackers and rotten apple core. "This car is disgusting," I said as we drove to the school, "no more food allowed!"

Stony silence followed my abrupt announcement. Then Emma went into panic mode. "I forgot my chapstick!" she yelled as she frantically scanned the contents of her backpack. "Mom, we have to go home!"

"We're barely going to make it in time Emma, we can't go back home," I said.

So, as we pulled into the parking lot of the school, they were both crying. The kicker came as they opened their doors to get out. You could almost taste the tension in the air. No one was saying goodbye. Just before they slammed their doors, Katie yelled out happily, "Bye guys, I'm gonna go home and watch cartoons now!" If looks could kill.

"Dear Jesus, thank you for our food, help me not to steal, and help a shark not to bite my arm off. Amen." – Ben Hughes

I'm *Not* Eating This

Have you survived a full-blown temper tantrum? If you've spent any time at all with kids, I'm pretty sure you have. They are the *worst.* I'm almost 100% sure that I would rather have a root canal than sit through another temper tantrum. When one starts, there's just no easy way out of it. All you can do is brace yourself, because the battle will be long and excruciating. And believe me: this is a battle you need to *WIN.*

My kids have all had their fair share of them. The trouble with temper tantrums is they usually come out of nowhere. They blindside you. Your usually sweet and caring child suddenly looks like they just stepped out of filming Children of the Corn. It's *scary.*

One warm summer evening this happened to me. The day had been wonderful, filled with bike rides, playing at the park and working in the garden. The kids seemed so happy. Things were going great. I should have known that ominous clouds were looming on the horizon.

We all sat down to dinner. When I handed Ben his plate of food he stared at it and then declared, "I don't like any of this." I played it cool and tried to ignore him. We all started to eat and then he mumbled, "Can't I just have some cereal? I'm not gonna eat this."

"Well, this is what we're having so this is what you're going to eat," Dave said sternly. Silent tears started to fall. Then the excuses came pouring out- "It's gonna gross me out!", "I have a headache!", "I'm too tired to eat this!" He pushed his plate away and crossed him arms in defiance.

I was at a loss for words. Everything on his plate was food that he liked. "Ben, are you hungry?" I asked him. He shook his head yes. "Then this is what you will eat," I said as I pushed the plate back in front of him. I locked eyes with Dave and we came to a silent understanding- the boy would eat his food. I took a deep breath and prepared myself for battle.

The girls finished eating and ran outside to play. That's when the wailing started. While I washed the dishes, I wore the earmuffs that Dave uses for firearms training. They are pretty good at muffling the loud screams of a five-year old. Every ten minutes or so I would walk over and ask him if he was ready to eat yet. The answer was always a very loud "NO!"

An hour passed, and then two hours. The tantrum raged on. I stayed strong, but only by the grace of God. I wanted to give in so bad. His sobs turned to whimpering, and then he just sat at the table in stony silence.

At 8:30pm (two hours after dinner), he finally started eating. He ate every last bite and then walked slowly over to me. "I'm sorry mommy," he said as he wrapped his arms around me. I carried him to bed and tucked him in. He was completely exhausted and so was I.

"This was not a good night, was it?" I asked him as I pulled the blankets up.

"Yeah, it was bad," he said sleepily, "but it could have been even badder."

"What do you mean?" I asked.

"Well, if you got shot in the leg with an arrow that would be worse," he replied as he drifted off to sleep.

I guess that would be worse. *Maybe.* The jury's still out on that one.

My Little Blabbermouth

School pick-up has not been going well, and I'll tell you why: it all boils down to the three- year old that lives with me. The problem started the very first day of school. Because her brother and sister were gone all day and she was bored out of her little mind, I took her to McDonalds. We had a really good time and she was happy to get out of the house.

But at pick-up time, she went all rogue on me. The minute Emma and Ben climbed into the car, she proclaimed as loudly as she could, "Sorry you guys didn't get to go to McDonalds with me today. I even got a toy."

I didn't make eye contact and held my breath. A couple seconds of silence proceeded the inevitable. "What? You guys went to McDonalds!" Ben yelled from the backseat. Emma looked at me in disbelief before whispering, "You mean, you went without....us?"

Oh, the drama. But it didn't end there. Every day my cute little adorable blabbermouth can't wait to spill the beans. Even when we do nothing exciting, she thinks of something to blurt out just as the car doors open.

"We got to go to the post office and mommy even let me put the letters in all by myself! And I got a lollipop at the bank, isn't that cool?" She is my Jekyll and Hyde.

"That's not fair! You never let me go into the bank with you," Emma whimpered from the back seat. Really? Has that ever been something she's wanted to do? I don't think so.

One afternoon, Katie and I went to the park for a picnic. As we sat there in the grass, I tried to explain that it wasn't a secret that we went to the park, but that we probably shouldn't brag about it. I told her that sometimes saying those things could make other people sad. She seemed to understand. We finished our lunch and had a great time exploring.

After we picked up Emma and Ben, she was unusually quiet. I thought we were in the clear- she was going to keep our little trip to the park on the down low. But as we walked into the house, she ran up to Ben and grabbed his hand. She said, "Don't worry, Ben, we'll go to your favorite park another day. You don't need to feel bad that you didn't get to go."

Oh my word. "What park did you go to?" Ben asked suspiciously.

"Your favorite one; the one with all the ducks," she replied with a small frown. "But mommy said not to brag so I'm just sad for you now."

So if you're wondering where Katie and I are these days, we're going to be holed up in the house folding laundry and scrubbing pots and pans. I'm interested to see how she spins that tale in her favor.

Be Still My Heart

We were cheering on the Fighting Irish at one of Ben's T-ball games. It was his turn to bat, and he walked up to the plate with a ton of confidence and a helmet two sizes too big. He hit a nice grounder past the pitcher and ran to first base. Everyone clapped and I yelled, "Way to go buddy!"

He gave me a thumbs- up and then yelled at the top of his lungs, "I love you mom!" My heart melted. He didn't care that his whole team heard him. He didn't care that it made everyone laugh a little. He just meant it- pure and simple.

Who's the Boss?

Dave, Emma and Ben were busy getting ready to go fishing. Dave was outside loading the poles, nets and rain gear into the car. I was busy packing them sandwiches and drinks in a cooler.

When Ben came running through the kitchen in just a T-shirt and jeans, I stopped him in his tracks. "You can't go out fishing like that," I said, "you need to wear your coat."

"Well, I'll go ask daddy if I need my coat or not," he replied.

"I can make that decision too," I told him.

"But Daddy's the boss," he said matter-of-factly.

I set the peanut butter down and stared at him. "Are you sure about that?" I asked.

He looked very uncomfortable as awkward silence filled the air. He shifted on his feet and tried to avoid eye contact. Then he said very carefully, "Well, you're the boss of the house, but daddy's the boss of fishing." Then he bolted for the door. The boy is wise beyond his years.

Me: "Why is NO ONE listening to me?"

Ben: "I WAS listening!"

Me: "Then what did I say?"

Ben: (long pause) "Ok, I wasn't *really* listening- just tell me again a little slower this time."

Spoken like a true man.

Full Circle

Before I had kids, I had *all* the answers. I knew what kind of mom I would be. I piously watched other moms lose control in the grocery store and I knew I would never do that. I told myself I would never go out in public with snot stains or food on my shirt. I would lose the sweatpants and brush my hair. My kids would look clean. I would remain calm. I would never stoop to bribery. My kids would *never* throw temper tantrums.

I would always shower and be dressed for the morning drop-off. I would never let my kids drink soda and they would embrace all kinds of food. I would keep my toenails painted and find the time to pluck my eyebrows. My kids would sit quietly in restaurants. I would never be that mom that has to drag her screaming child from the playground. I would be in control.

This fairytale came crashing to a halt the day we brought Emma home from the hospital. I'm not sure I've been in control since. I have broken every preconceived image I had of being a mom many times over. They don't send babies home with a handbook. You're on your own. And when those babies get older and start to have their own opinions? I don't think any self-help book can prepare us for that.

Some days I'm at the top of my game- I actually shower before we leave the house. My kids do occasionally eat all of their broccoli. Every once in awhile my nails get painted. And *sometimes*, my kids leave the playground without complaining.

But then there are days that I break every rule in my own book. One of these days happened three years ago in early December. I had rushed Emma to school in my pajamas that were stained with snot. My hair was out of control because we had slept through the alarm. And no, my toenails were not painted.

By eleven o'clock the house was a disaster and I still hadn't taken a shower. I gave Ben his Halloween candy bag as bribery so I could shower in peace. After my shower I instantly regretted that decision. A three- year old hopped up on sugar is not an ideal situation. There was no clean laundry so we wore dirty clothes. I had to call poison control because Katie decided to munch on a dishwasher detergent packet.

I was exhausted by the time we picked Emma up from school. But since it took us over an hour to get loaded in the car, I was not going right back home. We drove to a craft store to get some Christmas decorations. As I parked the car, Ben said he didn't feel good (probably from all the candy bars.) So, I carried him and Katie under each arm like footballs.

Right when we entered the store, Emma announced that she had to go #2. So, off we went to find the bathrooms. Ten minutes later we were still waiting for her in the hallway. Katie was crying and Ben was moaning that he wanted to go home. I cracked the door open and yelled, "Emma, are you almost done?"

"I'm trying to hurry!" She yelled back. I let out a sigh and leaned back against the wall. Then, I suddenly heard Emma break out into song from inside the bathroom. She was singing "This Land is Your Land" at the top of her lungs. I decided we didn't really need Christmas decorations after all.

On the drive back, I decided to stop and get some dinner to take home. I pulled Katie out of her car seat to find a major blowout- through her clothes and all. I seriously thought about giving up right then and there- just sitting down in the parking lot, staring up at the sky and sobbing my eyes out.

But I didn't. We bravely walked into the restaurant. Katie was wrapped in a blanket wearing only a diaper. Benjamin was dirty and whining. Emma was still singing patriotic songs and practicing her cheerleading moves. And I had not plucked my eyebrows that morning.

I caught the eye of a pregnant woman sitting quietly by herself. Her eyes widened at the sight of our crazy family. Two things went through my mind at the same time:

1. She feels sorry for me. Right this minute she is swearing to herself that she will never let her kids act like that! She is thinking, "I will never go out in public with my family looking like them."

2. She has no idea what she's in for.

Life had come full circle.

"Mom, I'm gonna be outside practicing my flips off of the rope swing- but don't worry, I'll be wearing my helmet." - Ben Hughes

Parting Words

It's two in the morning and I'm almost done writing this book. I'm tired. In fact, I'm so tired that I forgot to take Katie to school today. I'm serious- it never even crossed my mind that it was a school day for her. As I tucked her into bed, she said, "Mommy, it feels like forever since I've gone to school." Wow. What else had I forgotten to do? Did I even shower? I was pretty sure I did.

"I'm sorry, Katie," I said as I handed her Mr. Coyote. "Mommy totally forgot about school today! You can go to school tomorrow, ok?"

From the other side of the room, Ben piped up, "BTW, mom (which apparently means *by the way*), tomorrow is *Friday*- Katie doesn't have school!"

I shook my head and said, "Wow, I guess I need some sleep! I'm just talking crazy now!" They both laughed. They thought the whole thing was hilarious.

My point is this: We're not perfect. We're going to make mistakes as parents *all the time*. Don't be too hard on yourself- your kids love you even though you're not perfect. Now, I'm not an expert by any means, but I have learned some things (mostly the hard way) over the last ten years:

Enjoy the kids in your life, they grow up way too fast.

Stop comparing yourself to other moms (or dads). You're not them and you do what works for you.

Stop comparing your kids to other people's kids.

Once in awhile, it's perfectly fine to ignore the dishes and play Twister with your kids. I'm 99.9% sure they would rather hang out with you than have a clean house.

Pray for patience- we always will need more patience.

Laugh at yourself. And laugh with your kids. Life is so serious as it is; it will make you feel a lot better.

Choose your battles- and choose them wisely.

Don't lay in bed at night and think about all you did wrong that day. I'm serious- give yourself a break and remember the good moments you had with your family.

Cereal and Toast aren't just for breakfast- sometimes it's perfectly fine to have them for dinner.

Did I say pray for patience already? Pray for patience.

Don't go grocery shopping when everyone's hungry- that never ends well.

Wear out the knees of your jeans. God is always there to listen- *always*.

Share your stories- the good, the bad, and the ugly. It's good for the soul- and your sanity.

Made in the USA
Charleston, SC
08 March 2014